D1454220

YORK NOTES

Antony and Cleopatra

William Shakespeare

Notes by Robin Sowerby

Longman York Press

Exterior picture of the Globe Theatre reproduced by permission of the
Raymond Mander and Joe Mitchenson Theatre Collection
Reconstruction of the Globe Theatre interior reprinted from Hodges:
The Globe Restored (1968) by permission of Oxford University Press

YORK PRESS
322 Old Brompton Road, London SW5 9JH

PEARSON EDUCATION LIMITED
Edinburgh Gate, Harlow,
Essex CM20 2JE, United Kingdom
Associated companies, branches and representatives throughout the world

First published 1998
Second impression 2000

ISBN 0-582-32905-1

Designed by Vicki Pacey, Trojan Horse, London
Map by Celia Hart
Phototypeset by Gem Graphics, Trenance, Mawgan Porth, Cornwall
Colour reproduction and film output by Spectrum Colour
Produced by Addison Wesley Longman China Limited, Hong Kong

CONTENTS

INTRODUCTION

HOW TO STUDY A PLAY

Studying on your own requires self-discipline and a carefully thought-out work plan in order to be effective.

- Drama is a special kind of writing (the technical term is 'genre') because it needs a performance in the theatre to arrive at a full interpretation of its meaning. Try to imagine that you are a member of the audience when reading the play. Think about how it could be presented on the stage, not just about the words on the page.

- Drama is always about conflict of some sort (which may be below the surface). Identify the conflicts in the play and you will be close to identifying the large ideas or themes which bind all the parts together.

- Make careful notes on themes, character, plot and any sub-plots of the play.

- Why do you like or dislike the characters in the play? How do your feelings towards them develop and change?

- Playwrights find non-realistic ways of allowing an audience to see into the minds and motives of their characters, for example soliloquy, aside or music. Consider how such dramatic devices are used in the play you are studying.

- Think of the playwright writing the play. Why were these particular arrangements of events, characters and speeches chosen?

- Cite exact sources for all quotations, whether from the text itself or from critical commentaries. Wherever possible find your own examples from the play to back up your opinions.

- Always express your ideas in your own words.

This York Note offers an introduction to *Antony and Cleopatra* and cannot substitute for close reading of the text and the study of secondary sources.

> She shall be buried by her Antony.
> No grave upon the earth shall clip in it
> A pair so famous. High events as these
> Strike those that make them; and their story is
> No less in pity than his glory which
> Brought them to be lamented.

These words are spoken at the end of the play, which Shakespeare called *The Tragedy of Antony and Cleopatra*, by Octavius Caesar whose victory over the forces of Antony and Cleopatra at the battle of Actium has led to their deaths. He is conscious of his role in 'high events' and of his own 'glory' in bringing about these events. It may be that he is also saying that his glory, no less than their story, is pitiable – the utterance has an interesting ambiguity. However we take it, the two words which stand out, pity and glory, help to define what the audience feel at the end after the grand pageant of Cleopatra's suicide. The traditional account of **tragedy**, derived from Aristotle's *Poetics*, singles out pity and fear as the emotions induced in the audience by the spectacle of **tragedy**; we feel fear as we identify with the frailty and fallibility of the tragic protagonists and pity for the unfortunate results. Yet we also speak of 'tragic heroes' and this is certainly what we have in *Antony and Cleopatra*, a hero and a heroine of grand stature, whose deaths, whatever their frailties and fallibilities in life, might be said to celebrate a transcendent love affair that makes Caesar's success at the end seem something 'paltry' (V.2.2).

The story of Antony and Cleopatra would doubtless have been famous without Shakespeare; it has all the ingredients of the greatest interest: love, sex, a conflict between a public role and the desire for personal pleasure, power politics, high stakes, and a clash of cultural values in the union of a mighty Roman general and a sultry Oriental queen with a fatal result. But it is Shakespeare's dramatisation that has brought it vividly to life and made it for the English speaking world almost what the story of Helen and the Trojan War was for the Greeks. 'All the world's a stage / And all the men and women merely players', Shakespeare had memorably written in *As You Like It* (II.7.139–40). Yet his Antony and Cleopatra are hardly mere players; they play out their love affair on the world stage with a magnificence not possible for ordinary mortals. After he has left Egypt, Antony sends Cleopatra a rich pearl – 'a petty present' – with the extravagant promise: 'I will piece / Her opulent throne with kingdoms' (I.5.45–6). Later, Caesar complains that this is precisely what Antony has done in making her queen of lower Syria, Cyprus and Lydia (III.6.10). Was ever woman courted thus?

One of the greatest pleasures of the play is the magnificence of its poetic language which raises the characters in the imagination and sustains their larger-than-life status. Most famous is the picture of Cleopatra on her barge sailing down the river Cydnus to meet Antony (II.2.196ff.) which culminates in a statement of her 'infinite variety' (II.2.241). She herself grandly envisages Antony as, 'The demi-Atlas of this earth' (I.5.24), then continues her imperial vision in presenting her previous conquests of Julius Caesar and Gnaeus Pompey. Her dream of Antony after he is dead, 'His legs bestrid the ocean' (V.2.82), is similarly grand. Her response to the death of Antony, 'The crown o'th'earth doth melt' (IV.15.63), and her own words as she is about to commit suicide, 'Give me my robe, put on my crown, I have / Immortal longings in me' (V.2.279–80), sustain the regal note.

Shakespeare has endowed his strongest female character with great imaginative powers. She also prompts eloquence in others, whether they are praising or, more often, blaming her. She commands attention; characters in the play, audiences in the theatre and readers of the text cannot be indifferent to her and it is not only male spectators and readers who have found her rare combination of contradictory qualities fascinating and alluring. Queen and gypsy, poet and fishwife, witty sensualist and artful schemer, her words and deeds can shock when she strikes and harangues the hapless messenger who comes to tell her that Antony has married Octavia; and she can move the heart and touch the spirit when she responds to the death of Antony and prepares for her own death in the final scene of the play. She is one of literature's most vibrant, arresting and **paradoxical** characters.

Her 'infinite variety' is reflected in the play and it can be argued she is the dominating character. Few other dramas are made up of such varied constituent parts. There are the contrasting worlds of Egypt as place of pleasure and the more serious world of Rome, Rome being not only the city itself but also the scenes where Roman characters and Roman business predominates. Although it is conceived as a **tragedy**, the play is not uniformly serious and solemn. There are comic scenes in Egypt and aboard Pompey's galley when the Romans, too, show that they are capable of levity. The comic scenes have serious moments and undertones; there are hints of the ridiculous in the behaviour of the principals, or more often in the comments of their underlings, when apparently serious business is being conducted. This variety from scene to scene and the varied texture and tone within scenes may be thought to serve an artistic principle, in which variety is valued for its own sake as we might value it in a tapestry or in the composition of certain types of painting, but it may also express a philosophy of art in a deeper sense, an attitude that finds the division between comedy and tragedy to be an artificial one that impedes the fullest dramatic representation of life as we experience it.

This brings us to a general truth about Shakespeare, particularly applicable to *Antony and Cleopatra*, memorably enunciated by Samuel Johnson (1709–84). At the time, under classical influence, **tragedy** and comedy were kept very distinct and it was believed that Shakespeare was the supreme example of a dramatist who broke all the rules:

> Shakespeare's plays are not in the rigorous and critical sense either tragedies or comedies, but compositions of a distinct kind; exhibiting the real state of sublunary nature, which partakes of good and evil, joy and sorrow, mingled with endless variety of proportion and innumerable modes of combination; and expressing the course of the world, in which the loss of one is the gain of another; in which, at the same time, the reveller is hasting to his wine, and the mourner burying his friend; in which the malignity of one is sometimes defeated by the frolic of another and many mischiefs and many benefits are done and hindered without design.
>
> (Walter Raleigh, ed., *Johnson on Shakespeare*, OUP, 1908, p. 15)

Such is the play's variety that it does not have a single focus, a single great event upon which it is structured, a single vision to impart or a single perspective upon the love which might be thought to be at the play's centre. This leads us to consider some of the questions that the play has prompted among critics and readers.

Although it purports to be a heroic **tragedy** of love, there are **paradoxes** at its heart which have led some to question whether it can be called such at all. In the first place, is it love? For the unsympathetic Romans, Antony's involvement with Cleopatra is a demeaning affair of the flesh, mere 'dotage'. When he has decided to leave Egypt at the beginning, Antony seems to agree: 'These strong Egyptian fetters I must break / Or lose myself in dotage' (I.2.117–8). Does the play really allow us to say with confidence that the bond between Antony and Cleopatra really transcends the unsympathetic Roman view? In this connection it is perhaps surprising to reflect that, although they dominate the action, Antony and Cleopatra are not seen on the stage much together (they are kept apart by the world's affairs; this has dramatic point, of course) and when they are together, more often than not they are quarrelling or at cross purposes, misunderstanding or deceiving each other.

The only moments of harmony between them come intermittently in the war scenes; just before it they are at one in the fatal decision to fight by sea (III.7); after the defeat, Antony reproaches Cleopatra but when she begs his pardon he forgives her (III.11); when he thinks she has been flirting with Caesar's messenger, he flies into a rage, as a result of which she is forced to defend herself and he is satisfied (III.13). The most harmonious scene between them, which may be said to be full of unspoken feeling, occurs when she is arming him for battle (IV.4). Following victory here, he salutes her in the presence of his victorious generals (very little of their affair is presented in private). After the final defeat he blames her for betraying him (this time without foundation) in the strongest possible terms which he only retracts after he thinks she has committed suicide. As he dies, there is mutually reciprocated feeling (IV.15), but if they are the great lovers they claim to be they could hardly be at cross purposes in the face of death. Although Cleopatra dies to meet Antony, she also dies to defeat Caesar, and it is possible, though not necessary, to read her manoeuvrings with Proculeius, Dolabella and Caesar as a real attempt to evade the resolution to die that she makes in the immediate aftermath of Antony's death in the final speech of Act IV.

The grandeur of the lovers' passion is predominantly an effect created by descriptions of events that are outside the play's action: when Enobarbus describes Cleopatra's first meeting with Antony (II.2.19ff.); when Caesar shows disgust at Antony's enthronement of the Egyptian queen (III.6.1ff.); by declarations of feeling that are made when they are apart, in particular Cleopatra's speech to her maids, 'O happy horse to bear the weight of Antony' (I.5.21ff.); Antony's soliloquy in which he declares that he will be, 'A bridegroom in my death, and run into't / As to a lover's bed' (IV.14.100–1); and Cleopatra's dream of Antony after he has died (V.2.76ff.).

The same might be said of Antony's heroism. By the time of the action in the play it is a thing of the past, as Caesar recalls when he bids Antony, 'Leave thy lascivious wassails' (I.4.56). Although Antony is repeatedly called 'noble', apart from sending on his treasure to Enobarbus when he hears that he has deserted him, is there much in his actions in the play that really deserves to be called noble? What of his undertaking to Octavia, for example? In Act II Scene 3, he tells Octavia that he will behave; forty lines later after hearing what the soothsayer has to say, he has decided to leave for Egypt. There is much in his actions that is stupid, as in the case of his stubborn decision, against advice, to fight by sea, and much that is ignoble; nobody forced him to follow Cleopatra, 'like a doting mallard' (III.10.19), when she fled the scene of battle. The whipping of Caesar's messenger compounds this ignobility. After the final defeat, there is no reason for him to blame Cleopatra for a further betrayal in the savage and thoroughly ignoble terms that he does.

It can be argued, therefore, that there is a disjunction between words and deeds, that the characters do not live up to the ideal notions they have of themselves. Every reader has to decide the extent to which this is so, and if it is so to a significant degree, whether this is indeed part of the play's design or whether it is a weakness on the dramatist's part, that the play does not truly embody what purports to be its subject.

Some critics are not convinced that, although the protagonists lose the world, their noble love affair represents a transcendent value for which the world is well lost; they put stress on the political aspects of the play; after all, it does contain scenes that have nothing to do with the love affair, as when Ventidius arrives back triumphantly from victory over the Parthians and tells his fellow general that he will not seek further achievement because he is fearful of arousing Antony's envy (III.1). It has been argued that the play has been plotted to show us what is necessary for political success. It is not, of course, that Caesar is seen as an ideal figure – almost nobody has a good word for him; it is usually said that he is cold and calculating – it is rather the case that Antony's downfall is a lesson in political failure, whatever our reading of the play. To pursue the relation between public and private as it affects the protagonists will be a profitable line of enquiry.

PART TWO

SUMMARIES

'A booke Called. Anthony and Cleopatra' was entered in the Stationer's Register, an official list of publications, in May 1608. It is assumed that this is Shakespeare's play. The earliest text of the play is to be found in the First Folio, an edition of thirty-six plays by Shakespeare. These were collected together by two fellow actor-sharers in the King's Company, John Heminges and Henry Condell in 1623, some years after Shakespeare's death. Many of the other plays were also published singly in Quarto editions soon after performance in Shakespeare's lifetime. There is no Quarto edition of Antony and Cleopatra. Textual scholars report that the folio text, from which all subsequent editions are derived, is a good one, presenting fewer problems than some other Shakespeare plays.

References in this book are to Antony and Cleopatra in The New Penguin Shakespeare edited by Emrys Jones (Penguin, 1977 and reprinted many times). Readers who are using another edition will find that often the line numbers do not quite agree, and in some cases the discrepancies can be as many as ten or so lines. This is not because one text has more or fewer actual lines than another, but because they are counted differently. Any scene containing prose will be numbered to accord with the printing of the prose which will vary from edition to edition and in the case of verse different editors will count the half lines differently. Where a speaker ends in mid-line and another speaker seems to complete the line, if the number of syllables or feet exceed that in a regular iambic pentameter, the two halves will each be given a separate line number by some editors. Spelling and punctuation will also differ in varying degrees from edition to edition depending on editorial policy concerning modernisation.

Different editions offer different kinds of help to the reader. Most modern editions are prepared with notes. In the case of The Arden, edited by John Wilders (Routledge, 1995), The New Cambridge, edited by David Bevington (Cambridge, 1990), and The Oxford Shakespeare, edited by Martin Neill (Oxford, 1994), these are extensive and helpfully located below the text. The Oxford Shakespeare prints generous excerpts from Shakespeare's main source for the play – 'The Life of Marcus Antonius' in Sir Thomas North's translation of the Roman historian Plutarch's Lives of the Noble Grecians and Romans

(1579). In The New Penguin Shakespeare, extracts from Plutarch are usefully included where appropriate at the head of each scene or within scenes. Thinking about the dramatisation of Plutarch's historical narrative is an instructive line of study. The Arden, The New Cambridge and The Oxford Shakespeare also contain extensive accounts of the stage history of the play and of modern productions.

BACKGROUND TO THE STORY

Antony and Cleopatra is an independent play that contains within itself all that is necessary for the audience to understand it. Nevertheless characters in the play often refer back to their own past and to events in Roman history that took place before the play's action. First-time readers will more readily grasp the significance of what is happening in the play if they come to it with some knowledge of the immediate historical antecedents of the action. These antecedents had been dramatised several years previously by Shakespeare in *Julius Caesar*. Knowledge of the plot of the earlier play, which Shakespeare may have assumed in his audience, will serve as an illuminating context for what is dramatised in *Antony and Cleopatra*.

Julius Caesar opens with Caesar's return to Rome after his victory in the recent civil war with Pompey the Great (father of the Pompey who appears in our play). Caesar had pursued Pompey to Egypt (where he had been killed), met Cleopatra and had an affair with her resulting in a son she called Caesarion (mentioned in *Antony and Cleopatra*, III. 6.6). In the opening movement of *Julius Caesar* a conspiracy is formed, headed by one of Caesar's machinating lieutenants, Caius Cassius, who recruits the idealistic Marcus Brutus to his cause by persuading him that Caesar has ambitions to deprive the Romans of their liberties. Caesar is duly stabbed to death, ostensibly in the cause of freedom, on the steps of the Senate House on the Ides of March, 44BC (March 15 in the Roman calendar).

The conspirators justify their actions before the people but make the mistake of allowing Mark Antony, Caesar's close friend and henchman, who had not been part of the conspiracy, also to speak. In a famous speech ('Friends, Romans, countrymen, lend me your ears', III.2.75) he turns the people against the conspirators and they are forced to flee Rome. Antony is joined in Rome by Caesar's young great-nephew and adopted son, Octavius

Caesar, whom he had made his heir. They join forces to pursue the conspirators and defeat them at the battle of Philippi in Greece in 42BC (see Map).The action of the play ends with Antony pronouncing Brutus's epitaph, 'This was the noblest Roman of them all' (V.5.69), in apparent recognition of the purity of Brutus's motives in the conspiracy.

Antony and Octavius, together with Aemilius Lepidus, who had been a powerful political and military ally of Julius Caesar, had split up the government of the Roman world into three; an arrangement known as the triumvirate. Lepidus was given control of Africa, Octavius was in charge of Italy and the western provinces and Antony had control of the lucrative provinces of the east. Having conquered Gaul in the west, Julius Caesar had planned to conquer the Parthians in the east. Antony doubtless hoped to accomplish what Julius Caesar had been prevented from doing.

The action of *Antony and Cleopatra* starts when the triumvirate is under threat from internal dissension caused by friction between Caesar and Antony (as a result of Antony's distracting affair with Cleopatra) and from the external challenge posed by Sextus Pompey. It covers a nine year period starting in 40BC when the threatened rupture between Antony and Octavius is averted by the treaty of Misenum. After this Antony married his rival's sister, Octavia. The play then covers the disintegration of the triumvirate, with Lepidus losing power in 36BC, until the final defeat of Antony and Cleopatra by Octavius Caesar at the battle of Actium in 31BC.

The play ends with the suicide of Cleopatra, whom Caesar had wished to exhibit in a Roman triumph. Subsequently Caesar returned to Rome and celebrated a triumph without Cleopatra. In 27BC he took the name Augustus and reigned as Rome's first emperor until his death in AD14. He brought peace to the Roman world, establishing what is known as the 'pax Augusta'; this is prophesied in the play when he says: 'The time of universal peace is near' (IV.6.5).

SYNOPSIS

Act I starts in Cleopatra's palace in the Egyptian city of Alexandria. Two of Antony's soldiers, Philo and Demetrius, give a disapproving Roman perspective on what they see as the infatuation of their general with the lustful Egyptian 'gypsy'. Caesar's messenger arrives and is ignored. Antony rejects empire for love (Scene 1). As a soothsayer is telling the fortunes of her maids, Cleopatra enters, avoiding Antony who is now listening to the messenger. Antony realises he must leave Egypt for Rome and in conversation with his lieutenant Enobarbus determines to go (Scene 2). Cleopatra then uses all her wiles to keep him, but when she fails wishes him success (Scene 3). In Rome, Caesar complains bitterly of Antony's neglect of his military and political duties (Scene 4). Cleopatra, who previously in Antony's presence has been toying or wrangling with him, in his absence reveals the true quality of her feeling for him (Scene 5).

Act II deals predominantly with the political and military threat to the triumvirate posed by Pompey. The personal rivalries and animosities of the triumvirs are reported to him (Scene 1). In the house of Lepidus there is a tense meeting between Antony and Caesar in which Lepidus tries to keep the peace. Caesar's lieutenant Agrippa proposes that a marriage between Antony and Caesar's sister Octavia will cement their relationship. Antony agrees. After their masters have left, Enobarbus tells Maecenas of Antony's first meeting with Cleopatra and gives his famous description of Cleopatra sailing down the river Cydnus in her barge. He says that Antony will never be able to leave her (Scene 2).

Antony is seen briefly with Octavia, offering courteous words. A soothsayer then warns him to shun the presence of Caesar whose lustre will always outshine his. In a brief conversation with his general Ventidius, he determines to leave for Egypt, for, 'I'th'East my pleasure lies' (II.3.41), giving Ventidius a commission for Parthia. Plans for the departure of the triumvirate from Rome are discussed (Scene 4). The setting changes to Alexandria where Cleopatra, reflecting on Antony, is brought the news that he has married Octavia. In frustration and anger she beats the messenger (Scene 5). The triumvirs meet Pompey near Misenum, to 'talk before we fight' (II.6.2). They settle their differences and agree terms. Enobarbus discusses the instability of the new concord · between the triumvirs with Menas, Pompey's henchman (Scene 6). The triumvirs and Pompey celebrate in a banquet aboard Pompey's galley. Lepidus is carried off drunk, Caesar retires early, while Antony is the merriest of them all (Scene 7).

Act III dramatises the break-up of the alliance between Antony and

Caesar, culminating in war between them and Caesar's first victory at
Actium. Ventidius enters having triumphed over the Parthians. He is reluc-
tant to make further conquests in case he is seen to attract too much
glory to himself (Scene 1). Antony and Caesar part company (Scene 2).
Cleopatra questions the messenger about Octavia (Scene 3). Antony
complains to Octavia of her brother's treacherous treatment of Pompey and
his slighting of himself (Scene 4). Enobarbus announces that Caesar,
having used Lepidus in the war against Pompey, has now deprived him of
his command (Scene 5). Caesar complains to his subordinates about
Antony making Cleopatra queen of lower Syria, Cyprus and Lydia. He
shows a determination to stand up to Antony. He tells Octavia, who has
come as peacemaker, that, 'He hath given his empire up to a whore'
(III.6.66–7) and accuses him of preparing for war. The scene now moves to
Actium, Cleopatra insists on being present in Antony's camp in her
capacity as the Egyptian leader. Against the advice of his generals Antony,
who has the advantage on land in numbers and experience, is determined
to fight by sea where he is weakest. There is a suspicion that he is acting on
the advice of Cleopatra (Scene 7). Preparations are made on both sides
(Scenes 8 and 9). Enobarbus tells how Cleopatra deserted in the sea fight
for no apparent reason, to be followed by Antony who thereby brought
disaster on them all. One of Antony's generals deserts him for Caesar
(Scene 10).

After the battle, Antony expresses a deep sense of shame and
reproaches Cleopatra for causing him to lose his honour; he nevertheless
grants the forgiveness she asks for (Scene 11). Caesar rejects Antony's
ambassador, saying he will only deal with the queen. He sends Thidias to
try to win Cleopatra from Antony (Scene 12). When he learns of Caesar's
refusal to treat with him, Antony challenges him to a duel, whereupon
Enobarbus concludes that he has lost his judgement completely and contemplates leaving him. Thidias makes overtures to Cleopatra. Antony
enters as he is kissing her hand. He falls into a rage and has Thidias
whipped. When Cleopatra protests that she had no dishonourable intention, Antony determines to fight on, after, 'one other gaudy night'
(III.13.182). Enobarbus decides to leave him.

Act IV dramatises events surrounding the two final battles at Actium,
culminating in Antony's defeat and death. Caesar scornfully rejects
Antony's challenge to single combat. He orders that soldiers who had

recently fought for Antony be put in his front lines (Scene 1). Antony determines to retrieve his honour in the next day's land battle and generously acknowledges the service of his followers, addressing them as if for the last time (Scene 2). The soldiers in camp hear ominous music (Scene 3). Cleopatra helps Antony to arm. He goes off gallantly to battle (Scene 4). When news comes to him that Enobarbus has deserted, he sends his treasure after him (Scene 5). When this reaches Caesar's camp, Enobarbus feels acute guilt and decides not to fight against his former master (Scene 6). On the battlefield Antony's soldiers gain the upper hand (Scene 7). Antony jubilantly leads his troops into Alexandria where they are greeted by Cleopatra (Scene 8). In Caesar's camp Enobarbus expires through grief (Scene 9).

On the next day preparations are made for a second sea battle (Scenes 10 and 11). After his fleet have yielded to the foe, Anton denounces the 'Triple-turned whore' who has betrayed him (IV.12.13). Cleopatra enters but retreats in the face of his rage (Scene 12). She locks herself in her monument, ordering one of her servants to tell Antony that she has killed herself, with his name the last word on her lips (Scene 13). When the still raging Antony is told this, he decides to join her in suicide and calls upon his servant Eros to do the deed. Eros kills himself instead. Antony then falls upon his sword but fails to kill himself outright. Another servant enters telling Antony the truth about Cleopatra. He gives orders that he be taken to the monument (Scene 14). There, Antony dies in the arms of Cleopatra who laments his death (Scene 15).

Act V begins in Caesar's camp when news of Antony's death arrives. A messenger comes from Cleopatra seeking knowledge of Caesar's intentions. Caesar, revealing that his real purpose is to exhibit her in Rome in triumph, sends Proculeius with instructions to reassure her and so prevent her from doing anything rash (Scene 1). In the monument, Cleopatra's thoughts are on suicide when Proculeius arrives with reassuring words. While they are talking, one of Caesar's men, Gallus, breaks into the monument and Proculeius disarms Cleopatra of the dagger with which she attempts to take her life. Dolabella admits that Caesar intends to exhibit Cleopatra in a Roman triumph. Caesar then enters and threatens to kill her children if she commits suicide. He demands an inventory of her treasure. This she gives him, but her treasurer Seleucus reveals that she has kept back a significant quantity. Caesar, in apparent friendship, permits her to keep it and reassures her of his good intentions. She determines to thwart his real plans and orders her maids to bring her regalia. A simple Egyptian countryman delivers a basket of figs in which asps are concealed. She puts on her robes and crown, applies an asp to her breast and, rejoicing that she has defeated Caesar, expires with name of Antony on her dying lips. Caesar enters and in his eulogy orders that the famous pair be buried together (Scene 2).

ACT I

SCENE 1   **Roman disapproval of Antony's infatuation. Antony in conversation with Cleopatra rejects empire for love**

In Cleopatra's palace in Alexandria, Philo, addressing Demetrius, his fellow Roman officer, strongly denounces Antony's love for Cleopatra. He regards it as nothing more than a demeaning infatuation with a lustful harlot which is tarnishing Antony's former greatness. Entering the room, Cleopatra demands to be told how much Antony loves her. When an attendant announces that there is news from Rome, she taunts Antony that it is a summons from his wife Fulvia or orders from his youthful partner Caesar. Antony then dismisses the claims of Rome and empire upon him, asserting that love is the nobler calling. With his thoughts on the present moment he has plans only for the evening's entertainment and is not willing to hear messengers from Rome. Demetrius is surprised that Antony can so ignore Caesar and is sorry that his behaviour is exactly as common gossip at Rome reports it to be.

> This scene dramatises the central situation of the play in miniature. It is structured so that the love affair is seen from a Roman perspective and framed by Roman disapproval. The romance is shown under pressure from events in the outside world, represented by the messenger from Caesar, which will eventually destroy it. The scene in part bears out the judgement of the Roman soldiers about Antony, who is manipulated by the taunts of Cleopatra into neglecting his public duty. At the same time Antony's exalted language when he talks of, 'new heaven, new earth' (I.1.17) and speaks of, 'The nobleness of life' (I.1.36) suggests something more than a sordid affair of lust.

A sharp **antithesis** is established between Rome as a place of soldiers
and politics where Antony has until now been a hero of great heart
('plated Mars', I.1.4) and Egypt as a place of pleasure (I.1.46–7).
Cleopatra emerges as something of a **paradox**: a 'wrangling queen /
Whom everything becomes' (I.1.48–9, compare with Enobarbus's
account of her 'infinite variety' at II.2.241ff.). In the opening sentence
Philo says that Antony's infatuation, 'O'erflows the measure' (I.1.2),
exceeds what is moderate; this grand passion and its backcloth are
sustained by the language and imagery (see Language in Critical
Approaches). 'Let Rome in Tiber melt, and the wide arch / Of the
ranged empire fall!' (I.1.33–4). These lines evoke the grandeur of
Rome even while they reject it.

files and musters ordered ranks

office attention, duty, service

tawny front brown forehead, a slighting reference to Cleopatra, wordplay on
forehead and military front

reneges all temper renounces all self-control

gypsy gypsies were supposed in Shakespeare's day to be of Egyptian origin; it
is now thought that they came originally from India

triple pillar refers to Antony as one of the triumvirs; compare with arch at
I.1.33

strumpet's fool wordplay, both someone who is made a fool of by a prostitute
and someone who entertains a prostitute, like a court jester

bourn boundary

scarce bearded Caesar at this time he was twenty-three, some twenty years
younger than Antony

enfranchise set free

process a summons in legal language

homager servant

ranged widespread; ordered

twain two people

weet know

confound the time with conference harsh waste time quarrelling

approves the common liar proves what the gossips say of him is true

SCENE 2   **A fortune teller predicts the future of Cleopatra's maids. Antony hears of a succession of difficulties that need his attention and he decides to leave Egypt**

A soothsayer (fortune teller) is telling Cleopatra's maids about their future; his words are sometimes ambiguous and ominous. The women joke with him and among themselves. A first messenger announces that Antony's wife and brother have been stirring up trouble for Caesar, who has defeated them, and that Labienus, an opponent of the triumvirs, has successfully led the Parthians to the Asian coast. A second messenger announces the death of Fulvia. Antony pays her tribute and recognises that his 'idleness' (I.2.131) – which can also mean lasciviousness – is responsible for these disasters. He realises that he must break off from, 'this enchanting queen' (I.2.129). He communicates his decision to Enobarbus and in a final speech also reveals the threat posed by Pompey.

> The mood changes abruptly from the high drama and poetry of Scene 1. In the comic opening the women speak in prose; their humour is bawdy and largely inconsequential, though it is apparent that the fortune teller does not offer them the bright future they might wish. Cleopatra's observation of Antony that, 'He was disposed to mirth; but on a sudden / A Roman thought hath struck him' (I.2.83–4) marks a change of mood and theme. Again in Egypt there is mirth, banqueting and pleasure, while Rome represents serious business. Bad news brought by messengers (a frequent plot device) comes to Antony in quick succession; his seriousness, and therefore the gravity of the situation, is brought out in the contrast with the frivolity of Enobarbus who speaks in prose and continues in the comic vein of the scene's opening. Antony's final speech is businesslike and shows political awareness; it has none of the extravagant language he had used when talking to Cleopatra and shows that once he has made up his mind he can be decisive and focused.

horns   the old joke about cuckolding (adultery)
paint   put on make-up
liver   regarded as the seat of love
figs   ironic; the asps by which the women will die are brought in a basket of figs

cannot go cannot achieve orgasm

loose-wived married to an unfaithful wife

mince not the general tongue speak bluntly what everyone says

dotage infatuation, the word used by Philo in the opening line of the play

let women die let women experience orgasm, a frequent pun in this play

expedience haste; expedition

serpent's poison refers to the common belief that a horses' hair placed in water would turn into a serpent and also that a serpent did not become venomous till adult

SCENE 3   **Cleopatra uses all her wiles to persuade Antony not to leave Egypt**

Cleopatra sends Alexas to find out what Antony is doing, but not to let him know she has sent him. If Antony is serious, Alexas is to say Cleopatra is enjoying herself, if he is happy that she is sick. Charmian advises her against crossing Antony, but Cleopatra says that is not the way to keep him. As Antony enters she feigns sickness. She persistently interrupts him. He finally tells her of the business that necessitates his going. She accuses him of play-acting. When she sees that he is remaining firm and that she has lost, she wishes him success.

> Cleopatra reveals herself to be an actress of formidable range, feigning illness, turning Antony's words against him, taunting and perversely misbelieving him, while making false accusations to her own advantage. There is subtlety of interaction between the characters and their past and present when she reminds Antony of his past lyrical praise of their love: 'Eternity was in our lips and eyes, / Bliss in our brows' bent' (I.3.35–6). Is this sarcasm or nostalgic pathos? There is impudent irony when she says, 'play one scene / Of excellent dissembling' (I.3.78–9) for this is precisely what she is doing, and bold wit when, in response to Antony's anger, she scornfully accuses him of living up to the part of a 'Herculean Roman' (I.3.84). Shakespeare's source tells us that Antony claimed descent from Anton, a son of Hercules. Hercules was also a well-known dramatic character on the Renaissance stage, famous for his anger and fury. Yet there is dignity at the end when she apologises and bids him triumph in victory.

breathing utterance

our brows' bent the arch or curve of an eyebrow

a race of heaven of heavenly origin

scrupulous faction distrustful party strife

condemned Pompey he had been outlawed by the Roman senate

garboils commotions

vials small bottles

By the fire / That quickens by the sun that gives life

meetly quite good

target shield

The carriage of his chafe assumes the demeanour of an angry man

becomings graces; changes

Eye look

SCENE 4   Caesar denounces Antony and makes preparations to stop Pompey

In Rome, Caesar has received news of Antony's behaviour in Alexandria. He denounces it in conversation with Lepidus. A messenger arrives alerting them to the ever growing power of Pompey and his followers Menas and Menecrates, who have control of the sea. Caesar wishes that Antony might abandon his dissolute ways and return to his former greatness. He decides that it is time he and Lepidus take arms against Pompey.

The scene introduces Caesar, Antony's dominant rival. In what little he has to say, Lepidus is markedly more sympathetic to Antony than Caesar who speaks at length about Antony's weaknesses – at such length, indeed, that he emerges as something of a puritan. Yet he makes it clear that his condemnation is made upon political rather than moral grounds: Antony is imperilling the triumvirate. His behaviour reveals him to be a man of poor political judgement. Caesar, on the other hand, thinks clearly here and acts decisively; indeed, he makes no mistakes of political judgement in the action of the play.

The scene is skilfully constructed. Once again a messenger is used to propel the action forward with news of new danger. The threat that requires military action prompts Caesar to recall the active soldier of old; the tribute to Antony is moving and authoritative, coming as it does from his great rival. The picture of endurance and hardship that it evokes strongly contrasts with the earlier picture of drunken dissolution. The two pictures are opposites but complement each other in their extremity, befitting the characterisation of Antony who 'O'erflows the measure' (I.1.2). Antony is raised in the audience's estimation, while at the same time the Roman view of his character and behaviour expressed by Demetrius and Philo in the opening scene is confirmed and extended.

competitor partner, but with the obvious overtones of rival

Ptolemy Julius Caesar had arranged the marriage of Cleopatra to her young brother, who later became Ptolemy XIII

abstract essence

enow enough

reel stagger drunkenly along

stand the buffet endure the blows

foils disgraceful actions

lightness levity

the dryness of his bones a symptom of venereal disease

That only have feared Caesar that only remained loyal to Caesar through fear

discontents malcontents

This common body compare with Antony's contempt for 'Our slippery people' (I.2.186)

ear plough

Lack blood grow pale

lascivious wassails lewd drinking sessions

Modena in 43BC, immediately after the assassination of Julius Caesar, Antony was pronounced an enemy of the people by the senate who sent the consuls Hirtius and Pansa against him. They laid siege to him at Modena

stale urine

gilded covered with yellow scum

lanked grow thin

furnished ready

SCENE 5   **Cleopatra muses on the absent Antony, reveals her passionate love for him and receives news of him from Alexas**

Her mind wholly absorbed by thoughts of the absent Antony, Cleopatra wonders what he is doing and addresses him in her imagination. She recalls earlier love affairs with great men who adored her, Julius Caesar and Gnaeus Pompey, son of Pompey the Great and brother of Sextus who appears in this play. Alexas, who has been with Antony, enters bearing a pearl from, 'the firm Roman to great Egypt' (I.5.43) with the promise that he will make her queen of many kingdoms.

> After Roman politics, the change of scene to Egypt and theme to love is part of the play's variety, but the scene itself is greatly varied in texture and tone, reflecting the mood and character of its central protagonist. After Cleopatra's request for a narcotic so that she might, 'sleep out this great gap of time' while Antony is away (I.5.5), there are comic exchanges with the eunuch, revealing Cleopatra's emotional state and her sexual longing. When Mardian assures her that he has fierce passions and can think, 'What Venus did with Mars' (I.5.18), the mythological reference, indirectly alluding to Cleopatra and Antony, marks a change of register.

> Cleopatra then delivers her first great utterance of the play as she imagines Antony on his horse. 'O happy horse, to bear the weight of Antony' (I.5.21) is partly erotic in its suggestiveness, but also part of the aggrandisement of Antony. This climaxes in the allusion to, 'The demi-Atlas of this earth' (I.5.23) and continues in the military language 'arm' and 'burgonet of men' (I.5.24). The serpent (I.5.25) is an appropriate image to associate with Cleopatra given its ambiguous associations with treachery, wisdom and mystery. The 'delicious poison' of which she speaks in the next line follows on from the image of the serpent and expresses her consciousness of the **paradox** that she is indulging in conflicting emotions. In the rest of the speech she imperiously bids us reflect on her grand love affairs of the past.

> Once again a messenger is used to provide a change of focus. Alexis's account of Antony's offer of an oriental pearl and kingdoms to go

with it fully matches the grandeur of Cleopatra's imaginings. When she asks if he is happy or sad, then concludes, 'The violence of either thee becomes' (I.5.60), she draws an extravagant link between herself and her passionate lover. Her tempestuous passions are exemplified in her threat to give Charmian 'bloody teeth' (I.5.70) when, following her mistress's prompting, she praises Julius Caesar. Her extravagance is further revealed in her action in sending twenty messengers to Antony, and in the violent flourish with which the scene ends: 'He shall have every day a several greeting, / Or I'll unpeople Egypt' (I.5.77–8). After this scene, which in its language and style recalls the opening, Antony and Cleopatra, whatever their considerable flaws, are fully established as a larger than life pair involved in a grand passion that touches the sublime.

mandragora mandrake, a narcotic

unseminared gelded

What Venus did with Mars make extravagant love; Venus is the goddess of love (Cleopatra is compared to her at II.2.205) and Mars is the god of war (Antony is associated with him at I.1.4)

for wot'st thou for do you know

demi-Atlas Atlas bore the earth on his shoulders; demi meaning half – she evidently discounts Lepidus

arm and burgonet matchless in attack and defence; a burgonet is a helmet

Phoebus' Phoebus Apollo, the sun god

wrinkled deep in time like Antony, Cleopatra is middle-aged

morsel a tasty mouthful

arm-gaunt the meaning is unknown, perhaps battle worn

beastly dumbed silenced by this beast

posts messengers

paragon compare

ACT II

SCENE 1   Pompey contemplates the coming confrontation with the triumvirs

Pompey, boasting control of the sea and political popularity, is confident of success against a divided triumvirate, predicting that Antony will not stir from Egypt. News comes that Antony is in fact already in Rome. Pompey is surprised and discomfited but also flattered that his success has galvanised Antony, whom he recognises as the most effective soldier of the triumvirs. He concludes on a note of uncertainty; the triumvirs have cause enough to war among themselves, but fear may unite them against the common danger.

The scene forms a prelude to the meeting of the triumvirs that follows. It exposes political divisions and uncertainties in the Roman world. Pompey is clear-sighted about the weaknesses and rivalries within the triumvirate; he reminds us of Caesar's grievances against Antony, but also shows why he needs him. His opening confidence makes the threat he poses seem urgent. His vivid picture of the libertine Antony is dramatically interrupted by the news that the libertine, against expectation, still has the capacity for clear thought and swift action.

Once again a messenger is used to great effect, propelling the action forward with even greater urgency and showing in the reaction of Pompey that Antony is still the most potent force in the Roman world. Although realistic in his assessments, it is nevertheless ironic that Pompey is shown to be wrong in all his predictions: that he will be successful, that Caesar and Lepidus are not in the field, and that Antony has become so enervated by the bewitching intoxication of sensual pleasures that he will not leave Cleopatra.

Caesar gets money where / He loses hearts by taxation probably, which makes him unpopular. That popularity does not guarantee success is one of political messages of the play

charms of love the Roman view is that Antony has been bewitched, whether literally or figuratively

Salt Cleopatra lecherous

waned lip withered. Pompey continues with the moon metaphor that he had used when he said, 'My powers are crescent' (II.1.10). Actually his powers are about to wane

libertine one given to immoral pleasures

Epicurean cooks cooks for epicures or gourmets; Epicurus is popularly associated with the philosophy 'eat, drink and be merry for tomorrow we die'

cloyless sauce sauce so tasty that it will never satisfy. Compare with
Enobarbus on Cleopatra: 'Other women cloy / The appetites they feed, but she
makes hungry / Where most she satisfies' (II.2.241–3)
prorogue his honour suspend the operation of his nobler self
Lethe'd dullness the waters of Lethe in Hades (the classical underworld)
induce forgetfulness
amorous surfeiter this lover given to excess
'Twere pregnant they should square it would be obvious they should quarrel
among themselves

SCENE *2* The triumvirs patch up their differences and the alliance
between Antony and Caesar is cemented by Antony's
agreement to marry Octavia. Enobarbus describes
Antony's first meeting with Cleopatra

In the meeting of the triumvirs, Lepidus tries to keep the peace. Caesar
accuses Antony of undermining his power by causing Antony's wife Fulvia
and brother Lucius to make war upon him, of slighting him by ignoring his
messenger and of failing to meet his sworn obligations by refusing to send
him troops when required. Antony defends himself by arguing that Fulvia,
always uncontrollable, and Lucius were acting on their own initiative and
not at his prompting, that the messenger had arrived at an awkward time,
but that he had apologised the following day, and that his failure to send
troops was more a matter of neglect. He nevertheless offers a dignified
apology for failings.

Enobarbus reminds them of their present danger, whereupon
Caesar's lieutenant Agrippa proposes that they cement an accord through
the marriage of Antony to Caesar's sister Octavia. Antony readily agrees to
this political arrangement. They prepare to join forces against Pompey.
After they have departed, Enobarbus tells Agrippa and Maecenas about life
in Egypt and describes Cleopatra's journey down the river Cydnus in her
barge when she first came to meet Antony. He declares that Antony will
never be able to leave her. (The description of Cleopatra is discussed in
Textual Analysis.)

This scene may seem to fall into two halves without obvious
connection. But this is deliberate. Nowhere in the play are the two
contrasting worlds of Rome and Egypt so starkly and dramatically
juxtaposed. That the brilliant description of Cleopatra should come

immediately after the meeting of the triumvirs in Rome is a great stroke of art. If it had been delivered earlier, in Egypt, it could not have had the impact it has in this scene, where it suddenly injects the life and colour of an alternative world after the tense political manoeuvrings that have preceded it.

The contrast is also linguistic and poetic. There are no flights of fancy where Caesar presides; the language of the triumvirs is graceless and formal. Coming immediately after the proposal of Antony's marriage to Octavia, it presents us with the spellbinding magnetism of Cleopatra to which Enobarbus and, we know, Antony are bound to return. Quite frankly, after the hard realities of Roman power struggles, who would not find relief in the seductive charms of Egypt? The exotic picture of Cleopatra that emerges is not unlike the Roman view expressed before the meeting by Pompey, except that it is presented sympathetically. That it should come from the plain speaking and previously prose speaking Enobarbus is also a masterstoke. He had earlier refused to be diplomatic when pressed by Lepidus and had reminded Antony and Caesar that there would be time for them to quarrel after they had dealt with Pompey. His role in the play is partly that of truth teller. His judgement at the end shows that he knows Antony as well or perhaps better than he knows himself.

And speak as loud as Mars that is, speak contemptuously

stomaching resentments

curstness ill temper

derogately disparagingly. Caesar's language is harsh and formal

you were the word of war the war was about you

stomach desire

snaffle a bridle

gibe laugh, mock

your considerate stone Enobarbus will be as quiet as a stone but still have his thoughts

strange courtesies done unusual favours

despatch / We the business that is, make the marriage with Octavia: note that Antony shows no reluctance

a fly by an eagle a fly compared to an eagle. There is no suggestion that

Enobarbus did not enjoy himself in Egypt

pursed up put in her purse, took possession of

poop the ship's high stern

beggared all description made any description seem inadequate

Nereides daughters of Nereus the sea god, sea nymphs

yarely frame the office promptly perform the task

for his ordinary meal in an inn: the word ordinary is humorously chosen

great Caesar Julius Caesar

cropped bore a child (Caesarion)

riggish wanton

SCENE 3   Antony promises Octavia that he will behave well in
           future. A fortune teller warns Antony that Caesar will
           always be more fortunate than him. He decides to leave
           Rome for Egypt

After Antony's promise of good behaviour, made to Octavia in the presence
of Caesar, Caesar and his sister depart. An Egyptian fortune teller enters
and advises Antony to go to Egypt forthwith. Antony asks him whose
fortunes will rise higher, his or Caesar's. Caesar's is the unhesitating reply.
The soothsayer tells him that his guiding spirit, which in itself is
courageous and unmatchable, becomes fearful in the presence of Caesar,
who is sure to beat him at any game of chance. Antony dismisses him and
asks him to summon Ventidius, one of Antony's generals.

Alone on stage he acknowledges the truth of what he has been told.
Caesar has always beaten him in games of chance. He decides to go to
Egypt: 'though I make this marriage for my peace, / I'th'East my pleasure
lies' (II.3.40–1). He gives Ventidius his commission to act in Parthia
(against Labienus, see I.2.100–4).

Much happens in this short and pivotal scene. At the beginning
Antony makes a promise to Octavia and forty lines later he has
decided to return to Egypt. Did he make the promise with sincerity?
It is impossible to say. The use of the soothsayer cleverly makes it
seem that Antony is in the control of some greater force. The
soothsayer, who wishes to leave Rome, may simply have told him
what he wanted to hear to make him leave for Egypt, but what he says
is true to Antony's experience. This is a rare soliloquy from Antony in

the play. What is foremost in his mind, and therefore perhaps his main motivation, is not love for Cleopatra but the feeling that he cannot shine in Caesar's sphere.

office duties
demon daemon, guardian angel
hap chance
inhooped enclosed within a hoop or circle in order to make them fight

SCENE 4   **Lepidus, Maecenas and Agrippa bid farewell en route to Misenum to face Pompey**

A brief transitional scene that has the effect of keeping the main political movement of the play in the audience's mind.

SCENE 5   **Cleopatra beats the messenger who has come to tell her of Antony's marriage to Octavia**

While the triumvirs journey to Misenum, the scene shifts to Alexandria. Cleopatra is reminiscing about past pleasures with Antony when a messenger arrives from Rome. When he eventually tells her that Antony has married Octavia she beats him and even draws a knife. He flees in terror. She regrets the loss of nobility involved in her striking an inferior. He is induced to return to confirm the news. She bids Alexas ask him to tell her about the appearance, age and character of her rival. (Much of this scene is discussed in Textual Analysis.)

> The opening of the scene lightens the mood as Cleopatra recalls past frolics with Antony. The loss of control in her treatment of the messenger shows not only her tempestuous, even savage, nature, but also the true depth of her feeling for Antony.

billiards an **anachronism**, since this game was invented in Shakespeare's era and therefore not known in Cleopatra's time
angle fishing rod
betray deceive
tires and mantles headdresses and cloaks. Compare with Caesar's account of the behaviour of the lovers at I.4.5–7
his sword Philippan the sword which Antony had used in the battle in which he had defeated Brutus and Cassius at Philippi

formal ordinary, conventional

allay / The good precedence takes away from the previous good news

cistern pond

Gorgon the Gorgon is Medusa, the ugliness of whose face had the power to turn those that looked upon it to stone. The allusion is also to the perspective painting, showing two quite different images according to the viewpoint of the spectator

SCENE 6   **Pompey accepts the terms of the triumvirs. Enobarbus predicts the undoing of Antony's marriage and his alliance with Caesar**

Caesar asks Pompey if he accepts their terms. Pompey explains that he had opposed their power because of their support for Julius Caesar, who had fought his father, Pompey the Great, in the earlier civil war. He says that he came inclined to accept their offer of Sicily and Sardinia, on condition that he must rid the sea of pirates and send wheat to Rome, but that Antony's apparent ingratitude for favours that he (Pompey) had shown to his mother had made him impatient. Antony expresses his gratitude. When Pompey says he had not expected to see him there, Antony in turn thanks him for forcing him to come and for the benefits he has thereby gained. Pompey makes the agreement and asks for it to be sealed before they feast each other in turn.

Enobarbus and Menas, Pompey's lieutenant, reflect on what has happened. Menas says that Pompey has missed an opportunity and that his father would never have made such a treaty. Enobarbus agrees with Menas that Antony's marriage to the sober and dull Octavia is for the purposes of policy only and that he will go to his 'Egyptian dish' again (II.6.124). He predicts what in fact happens, that Antony's treatment of Octavia will be the cause of a breach between him and Caesar rather than a close alliance.

What is interesting in this scene in which the destiny of the world is settled is the inter-personal rivalry and point scoring. No great matters of policy relating to the immediate crisis that brought them into confrontation are debated. Antony's seeming ingratitude for the courtesy offered by Pompey to his mother and his occupation of the house of Pompey the Great are on Pompey's mind. Pompey cannot resist the temptation to needle Antony about Cleopatra and tactlessly mentions her previous liaison with Julius Caesar until he is stopped by Enobarbus. Caesar does not say much but is sharp and presses to a conclusion when he does speak. The conversation of the subordinates at the end confirms the sense of unease that underlies the human and political relations of their masters.

tall youth brave young men

factors agents

ghosted haunted. He came to Brutus on the night before the battle

To drench the Capitol with Julius Caesar's blood. The senate house where Caesar was murdered was on the Capitoline hill in Rome. (Pompey is referring to events described in Background to the Story in Summaries.)

unhacked edges undamaged swords

targes shields

composition agreement

Apollodorus carried refers to the story that Cleopatra was carried secretly to Caesar in this way

plainness directness, a characteristic of Enobarbus

SCENE 7   On board Pompey's galley, the triumvirs and Pompey celebrate their new found accord

The servants mock Lepidus for his inability to hold his drink and give the impression that he is a lightweight. When the principals enter, Antony has some innocent merriment at Lepidus's expense. Menas takes Pompey aside and offers to make him lord of the world by suggesting that he cuts the vessel's cable and kill the triumvirs. Pompey says his 'honour' prevents him from being party to such a plot; Menas should have done the deed without telling him: 'In me 'tis villainy; / In thee't had been good service' (II.7.74–5). Menas decides to leave Pompey. Antony is merry; Enobarbus orders entertainment and a drinking song. Caesar, who is not enjoying himself, has a headache and departs. Pompey declares that he is Antony's friend.

As the seriousness of the previous meeting between Pompey and the triumvirs had been punctuated by triviality, so the frivolity of this comic scene is punctuated by seriousness in the form of the projected plot of Menas. The scene casts Pompey's honour and his profession of friendship in an ironic light. He would have been quite happy to have seen Antony dead if this could have been accomplished without his complicity. In the previous scene Pompey had associated himself with the honourable Brutus and the freedom of the Republican cause for which Brutus murdered Julius Caesar. We now see that he would have been quite happy, if the conditions were right, to have supreme power himself.

The contrast in character between Antony, who enjoys good fellowship, and Caesar, who does not, is encapsulated in the exchange in which Antony bids Caesar, 'Be a child o'th'time' and Caesar replies, 'Possess it, I'll make answer' (II.7.98–9). Caesar departs with the observation: 'our graver business / Frowns at this levity' (II.7.118–9).

plants fruits of their agreement; footsteps

alms-drink the remains of drink left in the glass

pinch one another by the disposition find fault with one another as a result of their opposing characters

foison plenty

pyramises a drunken version of pyramids

held my cap off faithfully served

earthly Jove sole ruler of the earth – Jove (Jupiter) rules the heavens

pales encloses

inclips embraces

palled weakened

Egyptian bacchanals dances in honour of Bacchus, god of wine and revelry

pink eyne eyes made red with drinking

fats vats

Anticked made fools of us

ACT III

SCENE 1 Ventidius announces his defeat of the Parthians, but declines to go further

Ventidius, given a commission by Antony (II.3.42–4), enters in triumph having killed Pacorus, son of the Parthian king Orodes who had treacherously killed Marcus Crassus during negotiations in 53BC, a humiliation for Roman power. A fellow soldier, Silius, bids him make good his victory by pursuing the routed army through the Parthian empire. Ventidius remarks that Caesar and Antony have always won more through their subordinates than their own persons. He then points to the example of another of Antony's generals, Sossius, who fell out of favour after too much success in Syria, and says he would attract the envious displeasure of Antony if he achieved any greater success.

> The scene shows us the political world from the view of subordinates and emphasises the degree their leaders are governed by concern for their reputations. It suggests that there are limits even to Antony's 'bounty' (generosity).

> **darting Parthia** refers to the Parthian tactic of avoiding hand-to-hand fighting by flinging spears and then shooting arrows from horseback as they retreated
> **ambition** Ventidius is motivated by a sense of what is proper for his own advancement
> **that / Without the which** in other words, discretion
> **That magical word of war** Antony's reputation
> **jaded** driven like worn-out horses

SCENE 2   The triumvirs part company

Enobarbus and Agrippa mock Lepidus. Caesar bids a sad farewell to Antony and Octavia. Enobarbus and Agrippa reflect mockingly on the emotions of their masters.

> The opening sequence entertainingly suggests that there is little sincerity of feeling between Lepidus and his fellow triumvirs. Caesar is apparently sincere in his feelings for Octavia, to whom he is bidding farewell. The tearful Octavia has little to say for herself and emerges as a pawn between the two men. Indeed Caesar refers to her somewhat egotistically as, 'a great part of myself' (III.2.24). The remarks he addresses to Antony about Octavia serve as a clear warning. The mocking comments of Enobarbus about Antony's emotions at the end serve to suggest that all might not be what it seems in the present case.

> **sealing** fixing seals to the agreement

> **green-sickness** a form of anaemia supposed to afflict lovelorn girls. Lepidus's
> hangover is mockingly attributed to his love for Antony and Caesar
> **shards** dung patches between which the beetle Lepidus goes to and fro
> **band ... approof** as I would stake everything you would prove to be
> **piece of virtue** masterpiece of virtue
> **curious** touchy and particular
> **were he a horse** dark horses were regarded as bad tempered
> **rheum** watering of the eyes; Enobarbus is being sarcastic

SCENE 3   Cleopatra questions the messenger about Octavia

In what is an essentially comic scene, Cleopatra asks the messenger about
Octavia's appearance. Having been scared out of his wits before, he is
sensible enough to give Cleopatra the answers she wants and reports that
Octavia is dull and dowdy.

SCENE 4   In Athens, Antony complains to Octavia about Caesar's
           behaviour and starts making preparations for war

Relations between the triumvirs have obviously deteriorated as Antony
complains to Octavia that Caesar has waged new wars against Pompey and
slighted him in public. Octavia bids Antony not to believe all that he has
heard or at least not to take offence. She laments that she is caught between
them. He agrees to Octavia's suggestion that she act as a go-between. In
the meantime he determines to make preparations for war, blaming Caesar
for the rift.

> **semblable** similar
> **scantly** grudgingly
> **made his will** this probably means that he was courting popular favour by
> making the people his heirs
> **stomach** resent
> **branchless** maimed, that is, without honour

SCENE 5   Eros reports to Enobarbus the increasing power of Caesar

Eros, a soldier of Antony, reports to Enobarbus the news that Caesar,
having used Lepidus in the war against Pompey, has deprived him of power
and imprisoned him, and that Antony is angry that one of his officers has

murdered Pompey. Antony's naval forces are said to be at a state of readiness for war with Caesar.

This news is important in establishing that the reason for the breakdown in relations between Antony and Caesar is not primarily Antony's desertion of Octavia, for before that occurs, Caesar has been actively establishing his power.

rivality equal power

upon his own appeal upon the strength of his own accusations

thou hast a pair of chaps a pair of jaws, which will fight like dogs for control of the world

spurns / The rush kicks aside any straw

SCENE 6   **In Rome, Caesar denounces the personal and political behaviour of Antony who is now in Alexandria**

Caesar denounces Antony for publicly bestowing upon Cleopatra the kingdoms of lower Syria, Cyprus and Lydia (he had promised to give her kingdoms at I.5.45–7) and additionally for bestowing other kingdoms on her sons. Caesar then reports that Antony has sent accusations to Rome about him: that he had not given him his share of the spoils after Pompey had been deprived of Sicily, that shipping he had lent had not been restored and that Lepidus had been deposed. When Agrippa says Antony should be answered, Caesar announces that he has already done so, telling him that Lepidus had grown too cruel. He has offered to give up some of his gains provide that Antony gives him half of his. When Maecenas says he will never agree to this, Caesar curtly replies that in turn no concessions can be made to Antony over what he has gained from Pompey.

Octavia enters. Caesar remarks that she has come not attended by a great train in a manner befitting Caesar's sister but like, 'A market maid to Rome' (III.6.51). Octavia replies that she was not constrained to do so but comes voluntarily, having heard of Caesar's preparations for war and having begged leave of Antony for the purpose. Caesar informs her of what she does not know – that Antony has returned to Cleopatra. 'He hath given his empire / Up to a whore' (III.6.66–7) and has assembled neighbouring kings as allies. He bids her be patient, letting fate take its course.

Events are moving swiftly. The previous two scenes chart the causes of the war from Antony's side; this scene answers by giving Caesar's actions and perspective. Caesar emerges here as a commanding figure who plans, acts and speaks confidently and decisively. His assertion that Lepidus had grown too cruel is not supported by any of Lepidus' actions as presented or reported during the play and says more about Caesar than it does about Lepidus. The manner in which he feels Octavia, as Caesar's sister, should have come to Rome shows a proud and ceremonious concern for his own dignity. He does not mince words to spare his sister's feelings.

tribunal a raised platform

my father's son Julius Caesar had adopted Octavius, his great nephew

queasy the people are sickened by

spoiled despoiled, plundered

rated him allotted to him

an army for an usher an army to escort you, unusually extravagant language for Caesar

ostentation of our love its public avowal; a pompous ostentatious notion

on the wind speedily; Caesar knows more of Antony's movements than his wife

my heart parted divided; Octavia expresses no bitterness towards Antony

potent regiment ... us gives his powerful authority to a prostitute who raises a tumult against us

SCENE 7   **Arguments in Antony's camp and the decision to fight by sea**

Enobarbus tries and fails to persuade Cleopatra not to be present in Antony's camp, because he thinks she will be a distraction. Antony is surprised by Caesar's speed; Cleopatra contrasts Antony's negligence. Antony decides to fight by sea. Cleopatra supports this, but Antony's generals do not. His reason, 'For that he dares us to't' (III.7.29) does not suggest a considered strategy; in fact it seems rather childish, like Antony's challenge to a single combat (which Canidius points out Caesar has naturally declined). Enobarbus points out that Antony is unprepared by sea and much stronger on land, but Antony is obdurate.

News comes of Caesar's further advance. A soldier urges Antony to fight on land. Again he will not listen. Canidius remarks: 'we are women's men' (III.7.70), implying that Antony is in the control of Cleopatra. Canidius expresses surprise at Caesar's speed and the soldier tells how his strategies have deceived Antony's spies.

> Caesar's speed of action is contrasted with argument and confusion in Antony's camp. Against what sounds like good advice based on a strategic assessment of strengths and weaknesses from his generals, Antony offers no convincing reason for fighting at sea.

forspoke spoken against

denounced against us declared against us. Caesar declared war against Cleopatra as a foreign enemy, rather than Antony as a Roman

puzzle confuse

Traduced for levity censured for frivolity

muleters mule drivers

Ingrossed by swift impress hastily brought together by press gangs

yare ready

distract divide

is descried has been sighted

power army

Thetis a goddess of the sea (referring to Cleopatra)

Let th'Egyptians ... go a-ducking take to the water like ducks. The Romans owed their success to the land power of their legions

His power went out in such distractions his army marched off in so many different divisions

SCENES 8 & 9   The two forces are lined up near Actium

Caesar issues commands not to fight by land until the sea battle is over. Antony tells Enobarbus to set troops in sight of Caesar's battle lines.

SCENE 10   The account of the first defeat at Actium

A distraught Enobarbus reports the flight of Cleopatra's sixty ships. Scarus enters and tells of Antony's ignominious pursuit of her. Canidius, appalled by Antony's example, decides to take the troops under his command to Caesar's camp. Enobarbus, against his better judgement, says he will stay with Antony.

The defeat is put down, not to the prowess of the enemy, their better tactics or simply to bad fortune, but to the sheer stupidity of Cleopatra and Antony, their 'very ignorance' (III.10.7). When the fight was evenly balanced, or even slightly in Antony's favour, for no apparent reason Cleopatra flies, 'like a cow in June' stung by a gadfly (III.10.14). Antony follows her, 'like a doting mallard' (III.10.19). Cleopatra's fickleness and Antony's infatuation are the entire cause of their undoing. The contempt of their followers is expressed in their use of animal and disease imagery (pestilence, leprosy, nag, cow, mallard). Antony's behaviour is seen to be a gross betrayal of his manhood, honour and usual leadership, a terrible example that has prompted flight in others and causes Canidius to desert his cause.

synod assembly

cantle: segment

kissed away / Kingdoms the metaphor suggests the ignominious loss of empire for love

ribaudred wanton, lewd

The breeze upon her a play on two meanings of breeze – wind and horsefly

loofed having turned her ship's head close to the wind to make herself scarce

The noble ruin of her magic this is the ultimate proof of the Roman view that Antony has been ruined by Cleopatra's powers of enchantment (whether figurative or literal)

Did violate so itself Antony's loss of honour is a violation of himself for which he bears full responsibility

Been what he knew himself acted like his true self

SCENE **11**   A despairing Antony is visited by a penitent Cleopatra

Antony shamefacedly addressing his followers bids them take his treasure, hinting that he is bent on suicide. As Cleopatra enters, he reflects upon the contrast between what has just happened and the conduct of himself and Caesar at Philippi where Caesar had been a mere lieutenant and he had been the chief soldier. Cleopatra begs forgiveness for her flight, offering no reason, but saying that she did not think Antony would follow. He tells her she must have known he was completely in her power but does not berate or reject her.

This is Antony's lowest point in the play. He recognises that he has betrayed and defeated himself, 'I have fled myself' (III.11.7) and is in emotional, physical and moral disarray, 'for indeed I have lost command' (III.11.23). Nevertheless for the first time he is honest with himself, and he shows a magnanimity in his concern for his followers and in his forgiveness of Cleopatra.

lated   belated, like a traveller so late in his journey

mutiny   quarrel

doting   compare 'the doting mallard' in the previous scene and the 'dotage' of the opening line of the play

loathness   unwillingness

He at Philippi   Caesar

like a dancer   that is, by his side as an ornament

squares   troop formations, squadrons

is unqualitied   is beside himself

offended reputation   injured my good name

Thy beck   compare with Caesar's, 'Cleopatra / Hath nodded him to her' (III.6.65–6)

dodge / And palter   shift and prevaricate

shifts of lowness   using the tricks of those who are brought low

My sword made weak by my affection   the central **antithesis** of the play; Antony recognises the cause his own undoing

rates   is worth

full of lead   depressed in spirit

viands   food

SCENE 12   **Antony seeks to make terms with Caesar who sends Thidias to treat with Cleopatra**

Antony's ambassador requests that he be allowed to live in Egypt or, failing that, as a private citizen in Athens. Cleopatra asks that her heirs be allowed to inherit her crown. Caesar will not grant Antony anything. He promises to grant Cleopatra what she wishes, provided that she drives Antony out of Egypt or takes his life there. He then authorises his own ambassador, Thidias, to use virtually any means to make Cleopatra break with Antony and to observe how Antony adapts to his broken fortunes.

Caesar does not allow any sentimentality to interfere with his political interest. He shows a low opinion of women in his calculation that they are weak in misfortune.

Requires requests
The circle of the Ptolemies that is, the Egyptian crown
hazarded to thy grace dependent upon your favour
want will perjure / The ne'er touched vestal need will make the most virtuous break her vows (the vestals were servants of the goddess Vesta and sworn to virginity)
flaw broken fortunes

SCENE 13   **Antony has Caesar's messenger whipped. He determines to fight on**

In conversation with Cleopatra, Enobarbus puts the chief blame for the present misfortune on Antony; he did not need to follow her in flight. On hearing the ambassador's reply, Antony challenges Caesar to a single fight; the ridiculousness of this causes Enobarbus to conclude that he has lost his judgement altogether. Antony departs and Thidias enters to speak to the queen. He says that Caesar knows that she embraced Antony not out of love but fear. Cleopatra agrees. Caesar, says Thidias, would like to be Cleopatra's protector. Cleopatra seems to be complying. As Thidias is kissing her hand Antony enters and falls into a rage, ordering that Thidias be whipped.

He berates Cleopatra. She strongly protests her continuing devotion, to Antony's ultimate satisfaction. He determines to fight Caesar again by land and sea. They will drink and be merry before the fight. Enobarbus thinks Antony is attempting the impossible and that his judgement has completely deserted him. He finally decides to leave him.

This scene shows the less noble side of Antony; his treatment of Thidias recalls Cleopatra's similar treatment of the messenger in Act II Scene 5. The parallel serves to suggest a similarity in their passionate natures that are easily provoked beyond control. The beating of Thidias (and Antony's suggestion that if Caesar is offended he may beat, hang or torture his freed slave Hipparchus) is shocking and a further blot upon Antony's somewhat tarnished honour.

In mitigation, it may be said that his anger has its origins in genuinely deep feeling for Cleopatra. Her motives here and elsewhere are not entirely clear. Enobarbus is present for most of this scene and he comments on the action and judges the characters. His role here mirrors his larger role in the play up so far.

Think and die prophetic of Enobarbus's own fate

will desire, passion

ranges battle lines

the itch of his affection the craving of his sexual passion

nicked maimed

The mered question the sole ground of the dispute

the boy Caesar he is aged 32 at the time of Actium

Something particular some notable feat

ministers agents

gay comparisons showy advantages when compared with us (now that he has won)

judgement this opinion of Enobarbus perhaps recalls that of Caesar at I.4.33

square quarrel

a place i'th'story Enobarbus earns his place in the story because he chooses interest over honour and lives to regret it

under his shroud under his protection

in deputation as my proxy

I kiss his conquering hand is she flirting?

fullest best and most fortunate

muss a scrambling game. Just as Cleopatra had complained of the lack of ceremony (III.13.38), so Antony is angered by his loss of authority

tributaries rulers paying tribute

blasted withered, blighted

unpressed unslept on

a gem of women Octavia

feeders servants, parasites

boggler fickle waverer

seel stitch up. Antony recognises his blindness here

morsel Cleopatra had described herself as a 'morsel for a monarch' at I.5.31

trencher wooden plate

Luxuriously picked out lustfully selected

'God quit you!' God reward you, a phrase spoken by beggars

hill of Basan the fat bulls of Basan are mentioned in Psalm 22

The hornèd herd the bulls that graze on Basan or the men that Cleopatra has cuckolded

yare quick

fever thee make you shiver with fear

entertainment treatment

my enfranched bondman freed slave

quit get his own back

stripes marks of the whip

ties his points laces up Caesar's clothes

determines comes to an end

discandying melting

pelleted storm hail storm: the extravagance of the extended hail imagery impresses Antony; there is something **paradoxical** about the heat with which Cleopatra invokes coldness to deny it

buried them consumed them

earn our chronicle win our place in history

treble-sinewed, hearted, breathed like three men in strength, courage and endurance; overblown language

fight maliciously fight fiercely

gaudy night festive night

peep through show itself

There's sap in't yet there's life in me yet

pestilent scythe kill as many as death does in time of plague, characteristically **hyperbolic**

he'll outstare the lightning that is, he thinks he can do the impossible

estridge goshawk, a bird of prey

ACT IV

SCENE 1 Caesar rejects Antony's challenge

Caesar scornfully rejects Antony's challenge. His order to put the troops who had deserted from Antony into the front lines and his description of the feast that he allows his troops as 'waste' (IV.1.16) contrasts with the generosity of Antony towards his followers and his injunction in the next scene, 'Be bounteous at our meal' (IV.2.10).

falling the point of death

SCENE 2   Antony addresses his followers in the knowledge that it might be for the last time

Talking to Enobarbus, Antony determines to redeem his honour in the coming battle. He thanks his servants for their loyalty and service, bidding them treat him this night as when he was at the height of his power. He speaks of his possible death. When Enobarbus protests that he is unmanning them, he tries to change the mood, saying he was speaking for their comfort and promising to lead them to victory.

> The emotional pathos contrasts strongly with the assured calculation of the previous scene in Caesar's camp and with the violent anger which had induced Antony to beat the messenger. The scene shows Antony at his most human, introduces the theme of loyalty and lays the ground for Enobarbus's remorse for his desertion.

strike surrender or hit out. Antony sees only the second meaning

odd tricks unexpected actions. Like Cleopatra, Antony is unpredictable

Scant not my cups stint not the supply of wine

suffered obeyed

period of your duty end of your obligations

yield reward

Now the witch take me let me be bewitched

burn this night in torches that is, pass the night in revelry

death and honour the linking of these suggests that Antony feels that only in death (rather than victory) can he redeem his honour

drown consideration forget serious thoughts as we drink

SCENE 3   Antony's soldiers hear ominous music

Conversing together, a group of Antony's soldiers hear eerie music which they interpret as a sign that the god Hercules is deserting Antony. The scene forebodes inevitable doom.

SCENE 4   Cleopatra arms Antony who sets off for battle

The lovers put on a brave face to one another and to the world as Cleopatra, 'the armourer of my heart' (IV.4.7), helps Antony to arm. He is cheerful in his demeanour and actions, behaving, 'like a man of steel' (IV.4.33). Cleopatra is restrained and remarks upon his gallantry.

> **chuck** chick, a term of endearment
>
> **brave** defy
>
> **daff't** take it off
>
> **hear a storm** have a rough passage
>
> **squire** a body-servant or soldier's valet. Cleopatra is more efficient (tight) than Eros
>
> **The royal occupation** soldiering
>
> **workman** craftsman, expert
>
> **riveted trim** armour properly adjusted
>
> **port** gate
>
> **mechanic compliment** the fussy farewells of common people

SCENE 5   Antony receives news that Enobarbus has defected and sends his treasure after him

Encountering the soldier who had advised him to fight by land (at III.7.61–6), Antony admits his error. The soldier tells him of Enobarbus's defection. He bids Eros send all his treasure and write with friendly greetings and the hope that he finds no greater cause to change a master.

> Antony's admission of error heightens sympathy for him, as does his response to Enobarbus's defection. His generosity is prompted by knowledge of his own folly and by guilt: 'O, my fortunes have / Corrupted honest men!' (IV.5.16–7).

SCENE 6   In Caesar's camp, Enobarbus receives his treasure from Antony

Caesar gives orders that Antony be taken alive and that troops deserted from Antony should be put in the front lines. Enobarbus reflects on the fate of Alexas (hanged) and Canidius (ill received) who have gone over to Caesar. He already feels that he has acted wrongly before the messenger arrives with his treasure, whereupon Antony's bounty makes him feel acute guilt for disloyalty. He determines that he will, 'go seek / Some ditch wherein to die' (IV.6.37–8).

three-nooked three cornered, possibly a reference to Europe, Asia and Africa

olive a symbol of peace

vant van, front lines

Jewry Judaea

safed the bringer secured the safety of the bringer

continues still a Jove still behaves like a god (Jove was king of the gods)

turpitude baseness, dishonourable behaviour

a swifter mean a faster method; Enobarbus contemplates suicide if he does not die of a broken heart

SCENE 7   Antony is victorious

Caesar retires in trouble. Against expectation, Antony and Scarus enter wounded but jubilantly, and in soldierly fashion, boasting of victory.

     clouts cloths, bandages

     bench-holes holes of a latrine

     scotches gashes

     score cut notches in

SCENE 8   Antony enters Alexandria and triumphantly greets Cleopatra

Antony thanks his troops, greets Cleopatra and bids her kiss the hand of Scarus to whom he pays generous tribute for his part in their victory. She replies that she will give him a suit of gold armour. Antony, in a vibrant speech full of the sound of celebration, bids Cleopatra join him in a triumphant progress through the streets of Alexandria to the sound of trumpets.

     gests achievements

     Hectors the eldest son of King Priam. Troy's chief fighter, on whom the city depended

     clip embrace

     congealment congealed blood. There are many references to the actualities of wounds and fighting in these scenes

great fairy enchantress, a word with archaic and romantic associations

Chain my armed neck put your arms round my neck in a hug

proof of harness impenetrable armour

grey ... brown compare with the reference to his hair at III.11.13

Behold this man Scarus

carbuncled jewelled

Phoebus' car the chariot of Phoebus Apollo, the sun god

hacked targets battered shields

To camp to accommodate; Antony's response here may be contrasted with Caesar's feeling that the feast which his men deserve is nevertheless a waste (IV.1.16)

royal peril supreme danger

SCENE 9   The death of Enobarbus

After the fanfare upon which the last scene ends, the setting shifts in dramatic contrast to the hushed quiet of Caesar's camp on the same night. Two watchmen are reflecting on the day's defeat when they come upon Enobarbus in a state of acute depression. He poignantly addresses the moon, the 'sovereign mistress of true melancholy' (IV.9.12), as it is associated with mental instability and madness, and asks her to witness his repentance and asks for Antony's forgiveness. He does not seek to excuse his fault. He then expires. The watchmen take his body to the camp.

shrewd harmful

When men revolted ... memory when deserters shall be remembered with hatred

poisonous damp of night dampness that induces sickness; part of his death wish

disponge drop

being dried with grief the Elizabethans believed that grief dried the heart

SCENES 10 & 11   Preparations for a second sea battle

These two short scenes give notice that the coming battle is to be by sea; these are Caesar's tactics. Antony is confident to meet Caesar in any element. Caesar gives orders that a land fight is to be avoided unless Antony attacks. The implication is again that Antony's tactics do not match his other soldierly virtues.

SCENE 12 Cleopatra's fleet desert, resulting in a second and final rout by sea

Antony goes off to find out if the sea battle has commenced. Scarus then tells of strange omens connected with Cleopatra's fleet. Antony enters announcing that all is lost; he has been betrayed by Cleopatra (it is not clear that this is in fact so) and his fleet have surrendered. He vows revenge upon her and in his anger denounces her in strong terms. She enters but dare not approach him.

In the extremity of his anger Antony adopts the unsympathetic Roman view of Cleopatra, calling her a whore and a gypsy (compare with Philo at I.1.10). In also calling her a 'charm' (IV.12.16) and saying that she is a, 'grave charm / Whose eye becked forth my wars' (IV.12.25–6), he uses language that suggests the darker side of her enchantment. He later calls her a witch (IV.12.47), recalling Caesar's comment, 'Cleopatra / Hath nodded him to her' (III.6.65–6).

The identification of Antony with the mythical Hercules is well made when Antony says that, 'The shirt of Nessus is upon me' (IV.12.43). He sees himself being destroyed by Cleopatra as Hercules was destroyed by his lover Deianira. There is an ironic contrast between those scenes in which Antony is loyal to his followers and inspires their loyalty and this sudden change of fortune in which he sees his followers fawning to Caesar.

augurers those who interpret omens, usually by the flight and behaviour of birds

fretted chequered

Triple-turned whore! perhaps because she had moved from Julius Caesar to Gnaeus Pompey and to Antony

novice inexperienced youth

spanielled fawned

discandy become liquid

this pine is barked this pine tree (Antony himself) is stripped bare

whose bosom was my crownet, my chief end whose love was the crown and chief object of all I did

blemish Caesar's triumph spoil Caesar's triumph by killing Cleopatra so that

Caesar could not exhibit her in his official triumphal procession on his return
to Rome (see V.1.65–6 and V.2.109–10)

plebeians the common people

spot blemish

for poorest diminutives for the most insignificant people (whom Antony
imagines would most enjoy this spectacle)

Patient Octavia this is very much the conception on which her character is
based

The shirt of Nessus the centaur Nessus gave a shirt impregnated with poison
to Deianeira telling her that it was a love potion that would win back
Hercules's love. In fact it consumed him alive. Lichas, the messenger who
brought the shirt to Hercules was hurled by him in his death agony into the
sea

the heaviest club refers to the club that was Hercules's attribute. Antony is
contemplating suicide, an honourable death in the Roman tradition, as well as
death for Cleopatra

the young Roman boy Antony repeatedly stresses the youth of his opponent

SCENE 13   Cleopatra retreats to the monument

Afraid of Antony's wrath, Cleopatra seeks shelter in the funeral monument
she had built for herself. She sends Mardian to tell Antony that she has
committed suicide with his name the last word on her dying lips and to
observe how he takes the news.

Telamon when he had been defeated by Ulysses in a contest for the arms of
the dead Achilles, amongst which was the famous shield, Ajax, the son of
Telamon, went mad and killed himself

the boar of Thessaly sent by Artemis to ravage Calydon when king Oeneus
omitted sacrifices to her

embossed foaming at the mouth

rive rend, cleave

going off departing

SCENE 14   Antony attempts suicide

Antony is conversing with Eros when Mardian enters to give the message
that Cleopatra has committed suicide with Antony's name on her dying
lips. Antony orders Mardian to depart and Eros to take off his armour. He

asks Eros to leave him for a while. Alone on stage he begs Cleopatra's pardon and vows to join her. He summons Eros and tells him that his life after the death of Cleopatra is dishonourable and requires Eros to execute his promise to kill him. Eros refuses. Antony holds out the alternative prospect for them both of being exhibited in Caesar's triumph in Rome.

Eros asks Antony to turn away, bids him farewell and turns the sword on himself. Antony then falls on his sword, but fails to kill himself outright. Decretas and the guard enter, but refuse to kill him. Decretas takes Antony's sword with the intention of currying favour with Caesar. A messenger then tells Antony the truth about Cleopatra. He gives orders that he be conveyed to the monument.

The mistaken thought that Cleopatra has thrown in her lot with Caesar unhinges Antony: 'Here I am, Antony, / Yet cannot hold this visible shape' (IV.14.13–4). Then the thought of her suicide disarms him further: 'The sevenfold shield of Ajax cannot keep / This battery from my heart' (IV.14.38–9). The suicide of the loyal Eros raises sympathy for Antony who can inspire such devotion and is contrasted with the calculated prudence of Decretas in taking Antony's sword. With his life of a soldier at an end, 'No more a soldier' (IV.14.42), Antony becomes like a 'bridegroom' in his death and runs to it, 'As to a lovers' bed' (IV.14.100–1) with no subsequent reproach when he finds that Cleopatra has deceived him.

dragonish shaped like a dragon

vapour mist or cloud

black vesper's pageants the deceptive shows that approaching night puts on

The rack dislimns the cloud wipes out

knave boy, or servant

Packed cards ... triumph cheated in dealing the cards and treacherously allowed him to trump my glory; wordplay on triumph which can mean a victory and the official parade celebrating it, but also a trump card

She has robbed me of my sword compare Cleopatra's own boast that she has worn Antony's 'sword Philippan' (II.5.23). The Roman point of view is consistently that Antony has allowed himself to be unmanned by Cleopatra

The sevenfold shield of Ajax Ajax, a stout defender, had a shield made of brass lined with seven layers of oxhide

battery bombardment, a military metaphor

thy continent your body (which contains the heart)

Bruised pieces referring primarily to the armour that he is taking off, but also to his emotional bruising

seal finish

Eros! – I come, my Queen – Eros! in classical mythology, Eros is the god of love

Dido and Aeneas mythical lovers, not actually united after death, since Dido did not forgive Aeneas for deserting her to go and found Rome. Is this Shakespeare's mistake or Antony's? It is characteristic of the desire of the protagonists to see themselves in grand mythical terms

Quartered divided up

exigent final emergency

inevitable prosecution unavoidable pursuit

windowed placed as in a window

with pleached arms with hands bound behind him

wheeled seat chariot

brave instruction courageous example

got upon me a nobleness in record have beaten me in winning a noble place in history

SCENE 15 Antony dies in Cleopatra's arms

Antony is brought to the monument. Cleopatra will not come down because she fears that she will be captured. Thus he has to be hoisted up. Antony, selfless in death and concerned for her safety, bids her trust no-one about Caesar but Proculeius. Cleopatra replies that she will put her trust in her own hands. Antony pronounces his own epitaph: 'a Roman, by a Roman / Valiantly vanquished' (IV.15.57). On his death Cleopatra faints, then movingly laments his passing. (This is discussed in Textual Analysis.)

Not Caesar's valour Antony's valour has triumphed by virtue of his suicide, regarded as an act of self-control by the Romans

full-fortuned victorious, favoured by fortune, lucky

Be brooched with me be ornamented with me

Demuring looking at me demurely; the picture of Octavia is that of the dignified and sober, if slightly complacent, Roman matron

Here's sport indeed ironic

heaviness literally, weight and also meaning grief

Juno wife of Jove, the most powerful of the classical goddesses

Mercury the messenger of the gods
The soldier's pole perhaps the pole star, a standard or a maypole
chares chores
sottish stupid
Good sirs addressed to her women

ACT V

SCENE 1   **Caesar hears of Antony's death. He assures an Egyptian messenger of his goodwill towards Cleopatra**

Decretas enters Caesar's camp with news of Antony's suicide. Caesar weeps and pays him tribute. His tribute is interrupted by the arrival of a messenger from Cleopatra seeking to know his intentions. Caesar courteously reassures him that she will be treated honourably. After he has departed, he gives instructions to Proculeius to allay her fears, lest she kill herself and deprive him of her part in his Roman triumph. He sends Gallus after him.

The words of Decretas and the tribute of Caesar continue to uphold the dignity of Antony even if the tone is less exalted. Decretas is, after all, changing sides and Maecenas perceptively remarks that Caesar's tears are the consequence of seeing his own fate potentially mirrored in that of Antony. In command and efficient as ever, Caesar is not so overcome by the news that he allows feelings of sorrow (or triumph) to interfere with the business of the moment, so that the interrupting messenger is dealt with straightaway. Once again his response is above all political: he will do anything to ensure that Cleopatra survives to grace his triumphant return to Rome.

his haters those who hate him
shook lions into civil streets Caesar, in **hyperbolic** language, suggests that Antony's death should have produced the prodigious effects that were supposed to have followed the death of Julius Caesar, when lions were reported on the streets of Rome
doom death
moiety half
The gods rebuke me because he is shedding tears
launch lance

stall live
In top of all design in worthiest enterprise
meeter season more appropriate time
intents intentions
by some of ours through some of our representatives
quality of her passion the nature of her grief
her life in Rome ... triumph her presence in Rome at my triumph would immortalise it
hardly reluctantly

SCENE 2   Cleopatra commits suicide to defeat Caesar and join Antony

This long scene may be regarded as having three movements. In the first Cleopatra explores Caesar's intentions towards her and comes to suspect what they are. In the second, through gaining Dolabella's sympathy, she becomes certain in her knowledge; there is nothing in her meeting with Caesar to make her think otherwise and on Caesar's departure Dolabella is even more specific. In the third she acts to defeat these intentions.

Cleopatra enters with her thoughts on suicide. Proculeius then enters with reassuring words; if she accepts his authority, Caesar will take heed of her wishes. Cleopatra hopes for her kingdom, or failing that, for her son to inherit and agrees to meet him. Gallus enters and disarms her of the dagger which she draws. Her compliant attitude changes after his intervention.

Gallus bids Proculeius guard her. In ambiguous words the latter begs her not to, 'abuse my master's bounty by / Th'undoing of yourself. Let the world see / His nobleness well acted' (V.2.43–5). Proculeius doubtless means Cleopatra to understand that Caesar is concerned that his reputation for clemency and magnanimity will be harmed by her suicide. She rightly suspects another meaning, that Caesar wishes to keep her alive so that he can make a theatrical spectacle of her in a glorious Roman triumph, a fate that the queen judges to be worse than death.

Dolabella enters and takes over from Proculeius. She tells Dolabella of her grandly imagined dream of Antony: 'His delights / Were dolphin-like' and so forth (V.2.88–9). Dolabella is moved by her words and tells her what she desires to know, that Caesar intends to lead her in triumph. Caesar then enters and treats Cleopatra with diplomatic authority. She is dignified in offering her obeisance, handing him an account of her treasure and monies. She bids her treasurer Seleucus ratify its contents, but when he says that she has kept back as much as she has declared, she is greatly humiliated, though Caesar professes to admire her prudence in making provision for herself and allows her to keep it, departing in peace.

It is not clear whether she kept back this treasure because she wished to fool Caesar into thinking that she wants to live or whether she really did want to live. After he has gone, she shows that she has taken the measure of Caesar judging him to be all words and her whispers to Charmian, to judge from Charmian's reply, concern arrangements to be made for her suicide. Dolabella enters and tells her of Caesar's arrangements: Caesar will journey through Syria; within three days she and her children will be sent on ahead.

Convinced that she will become part of a Roman pageant, Cleopatra now determines to defeat Caesar's purposes, bidding Charmian fetch all her regalia for her final scene. A guardsman enters with simple rustic character carrying a basket of figs, in which are concealed the asps whose poison will provide the means of release. Charmian returns with her regalia. Cleopatra dons her regal robes, 'Give me my robe; put on my crown; I have / Immortal longings in me' (V.2.279–80). She bids farewell to her maids, who share her fate, and expires with Antony's name on her dying lips. Dolabella enters to discover them, followed by Caesar, who pronounces their epitaph.

> Fully sure of Caesar's intentions to make a vulgar theatrical exhibition of her in his Roman triumph, Cleopatra contrives her own regal pageant by which she will defeat his purposes and retain her dignity; her death is, in fact, is accompanied by the ceremonial ritual associated with a coronation. Before the end, while she is treating with Caesar and his lieutenants, she shows evidence of the fiery temper and strong language she has previously exhibited and in her dream of Antony provides contrary evidence of her grand imaginative power and poetic ability.

> Lesser characters have their part to play in the grand climax; the clown, with his verbal fumbling and bawdy innuendo injects a comic note (the incongruity of which only serves to heighten tension), while

her maidservants in their loyalty and affection help both to give a human touch and to exalt Cleopatra in Charmian's touching tribute as a 'lass unparalleled' (V.2.315).

a better life that is, gives her a better perspective on life, a Stoic perspective in which the individual despises the gifts of fortune and triumphs over bad fortune by virtue of inner strength and resolution

knave servant

that thing suicide

palates more the dung tastes again the base product of earth (dung) which nourishes the poorest and the most powerful

Antony ... bade me trust you at IV.15.48; another bad political judgement on Antony's part; it is Dolabella not Proculeius who tells her the truth

majesty, to keep decorum to do what is appropriate to majesty; despite her impulsiveness, Cleopatra never loses sight of her regal status and the respect it entails

grace goodwill

sweet dependency willing submission to his authority

his fortune's vassal the servant of his success; she acknowledges his authority

rids our dogs of languish puts an end to the lingering diseases of dogs

worth many babes and beggars! those to whom death most readily comes

pinioned with arms tied behind, or with clipped wings

shouting varletry the noisy common people

Blow me into abhorring lay eggs upon me and make me repellent

your trick your habit

bestrid straddled

his reared arm / Crested the world his raised arm dominated the world

propertied ... spheres endowed with the heavenly music of the spheres

quail make quail or quake

His delights ... lived in just as dolphins show their backs above the water that is the element in which they live, so Antony rose above the pleasures that were his element

In his livery in his service

crowns and crownets kings and princes

plates coins

It's past the size of dreaming no mere dream could equal the reality

fancy the imagination

Condemning shadows quite entirely discrediting the shadowy figments of the imagination; in what is said about nature and fancy this speech about Antony bears similarities with Enobarbus's speech about Cleopatra at II.2.195ff

written in our flesh shown in our war wounds

frailties which before / Have often shamed our sex in this, Cleopatra may not be sincere, but it is significant that she does not seek to put the blame on Antony

enforce emphasise

lay on me a cruelty make me look cruel in the eyes of the world; Caesar is concerned about what in the modern world would be called his image

your children in threatening these Caesar shows his true political colours

scutcheons shields showing coats of arms

brief summary list

How pomp is followed how power (Caesar's) is courted

Immoment toys unimportant trivialities

the cinders of my spirits / Through the ashes of my chance the living fire of my spirit which is concealed beneath my burnt out fortunes; she does, in fact, show in this exchange some of her old fire

Make not your thoughts your prisons do not think you are a prisoner

Be noble to myself do the honourable thing, that is commit suicide

my love makes religion to obey my regard for you makes it a matter of duty to obey; Dolabella seems to have fallen under Cleopatra's spell

puppet as in a show; Cleopatra imagines being exhibited in an Egyptian tableau for the entertainment of the common people

Mechanic engaged in manual work, working class

Rank of gross diet smelling of bad food

Saucy lictors insolent (perhaps lascivious) officers of magistrates

scald rhymers / Ballad us out o' tune contemptible poets shall sing our story in ballads

Extemporally in impromptu performances

Some squeaking Cleopatra boy my greatness some incompetent boy actor reduce my greatness; this line prompts thought about the actual performance of the part on the Jacobean stage

Cydnus the river down which she had sailed in her barge when first she met Antony

marble-constant as unchanging as marble

the fleeting moon the moon as it waxes and wanes is a symbol of inconstancy. Earlier Cleopatra had appeared in the costume of the Egyptian moon goddess, Isis, at III.6.16–9

worm of Nilus the snake of the Nile, the asp

immortal the clown means mortal

given to lie to tell a lie, or to lie with men

falliable he means infallible

Immortal longings longs for immortality

yare quick

other elements earth and water

aspic the poison of the asp

curled Antony carefully barbered. When they first met Antony was 'barbered ten times o'er' (II.2.229)

intrinsicate mysteriously intricate

dispatch end it quickly

Ass / Unpolicied a fool outwitted in his policy

Downy windows eyelids as soft as down

awry crooked

Touch their effects reach their expected results

She levelled at our purposes she guessed our intentions

in her strong toil of grace in the powerful snare of her beauty

something blown something swollen

clip embrace

solemnity ceremonious occasion

PART THREE

CRITICAL APPROACHES

THE STRUCTURE OF THE PLOT

The folio text does not contain act divisions, but it does provide stage directions and indications of scene settings from which a reliable sequence can be established; act divisions were provided by Shakespeare's first editors in the eighteenth century. This early division of the play into acts and scenes has generally been accepted, though it should be noted that in The Oxford Shakespeare Agrippa's three line utterance at the beginning of IV.7 is counted as a separate scene, so that in this edition there are sixteen scenes in Act IV. The usual total of forty-two scenes is considerably more than in any other play by Shakespeare and tells us something of his technique in *Antony and Cleopatra*.

The play is marked by a distinct **antithetical** structure. In the first half before the movement towards Actium, there is the contrast between scenes in Egypt and the political scenes in which Roman business is conducted. Act I is set mostly in Egypt, with a contrasting scene in Caesar's house (I.4) in which Caesar expresses his disapproval of Antony's doings in Egypt; Act II, which covers the Roman business with Pompey, is interrupted by one scene in Egypt (II.5) in which Cleopatra beats the messenger who has come to tell her of Antony's marriage to Octavia. Act III opens with Ventidius on the plains of Syria, returns to Rome for the parting of the triumvirs, switches to Egypt to see Cleopatra asking about Octavia, then goes to Antony's house in Athens for two scenes of political business, returning to Rome for further political business as the triumvirate breaks up before moving to Actium for Scene 7.

Here at the halfway point the scene setting follows the logic of the action, moving between Actium and Cleopatra's palace in Alexandria. Where the **antithesis** before Actium had been between Egypt and Roman business (the private world of Antony and Cleopatra and the public world of Roman politics), after Actium the **antithesis** is between what is happening in Antony's camp and what is happening in Caesar's camp.

> The continual hurry of the action, the variety of incidents, and the quick succession
> of one personage after another, call the mind forward without intermission from the
> first act to the last. But the power of delighting is derived principally from the
> frequent changes of the scene.
>
> (Walter Raleigh, ed., *Johnson on Shakespeare*, OUP, 1908, p. 180)

To Samuel Johnson's verdict here, we may add that this juxtapositioning is a highly effective way of dramatising the split in Antony's public and private life and the consequences that this split entails in his conflict with Caesar. Thus the dramatic form or structure that Shakespeare has chosen reflects the major thematic concerns of the play.

To some extent this form is that of a chronicle play, that is a play that follows a broad sequence of events, often covering a long period of time (over ten years in the case of this play) in a straightforward chronological order. Yet this is not entirely true because Shakespeare has begun in the middle of things, after Antony has got into political difficulties as a result of his affair with Cleopatra. Enobarbus's description of the lovers' first meeting (II.2.195ff.) is a kind of retrospective narrative, though we hardly notice it as such. Similar is Caesar's praise of Antony's past exploits as a general. The point at which Shakespeare has chosen to begin indicates the main theme.

The structure of the play has not always been admired. Here is Samuel Johnson's verdict: 'The events, of which the principal are described according to history, are produced without any art of connection or care of disposition.' Close examination of the play in relation to that history (that is, principally the account found in Plutarch's 'Life of Antony') reveals this verdict to be an exaggeration, to say the least.

In the first place there are omissions; for example, Antony's disastrous Parthian campaigns, in which it is estimated that he lost over 30,000 troops, are not to Shakespeare's purpose, there are enough disasters without these. Antony's life with Octavia, which produced several children, is omitted. Then there are changes to the source ('care of disposition') and inventions. For example, Cleopatra beats her treasurer Seleucus in Plutarch but the scene in which she beats the messenger who tells her of Antony's marriage to Octavia is an invention. Enobarbus is mentioned incidentally in Plutarch but the development of his character and role (see Characterisation) is a major Shakespearean invention which, amongst other things, gives coherence ('art of connection') to the plot.

Yet there are inherent difficulties in the chronicle approach. So much history has to be crammed into a short compass that there are gaps and omissions, omissions of things that, quite irrespective of any historical account, in the dramatisation of the events of the play we may legitimately wish to know. For example, when Antony promises Octavia to behave himself, is he at this moment sincere? (Consider that forty lines later he says that he has made the marriage for his peace and is leaving for the east in which his pleasure lies.) What was in Caesar's mind in allowing the one person he seems to care about to marry Antony? We have no way of knowing; the treatment of this stage of the story is quite superficial. Often we do not know as much as we might like to know about the motivation of the characters. Significantly, the play has few soliloquies, the place on the Renaissance stage where we might find motives explored and inner conflicts expressed.

The broad sweep of the chronicle often precludes depth. But the fast moving juxtaposition of scenes involving a vast number of characters compensates for any lack of depth by giving us complexity of a different sort; events are seen from a variety of perspectives to give us not simply a narrative sequence mostly from one point of view, as in Plutarch, but an active sense of history being made and destinies being determined from the interaction of competing forces, both personal and more broadly political. *Julius Caesar* centres upon the build up to, and consequences of, a single event (the assassination of Caesar). In contrast to this **unity** of action, in *Antony and Cleopatra* there is no particular dominant action but rather many events, both public and private, that follow on from what the Romans at the beginning of the play see as Antony's 'dotage'. The play derives what **unity** it has not from action or even from character but from this over-arching theme.

CHARACTERISATION

The characterisations of Antony, Cleopatra and Octavius Caesar follow quite closely the portraits of them in Plutarch, except that Shakespeare has presented the lovers more attractively, whilst the opposite is true of Caesar. In Plutarch, though Antony is magnanimous, bountiful, courageous, and convivial, he is also cruel, lecherous and corrupt. Shakespeare's Antony is far more noble. Cleopatra is perhaps surprisingly well presented in Plutarch as enchanting and exotic (see Textual Analysis) and also intelligent; the intense realisation of her as a **paradoxical** union of contradictory qualities is Shakespeare's own response to what he found in his source. Shakespeare has conceived Octavius very much as Antony's opposite; whereas in Plutarch he is said to have a weakness for women, in Shakespeare he is abstemious, censorious and cold. His political virtues are presented by the dramatist in such a way that they almost suggest a human limitation.

The principal characters are the subject of comment in the notes that follow the summaries, while the presentation of the lovers, particularly of Cleopatra, is discussed in detail in Textual Analysis. Shakespeare's dramatic construction and design will be illustrated here with reference to what is Shakespeare's single most striking invention, his development of the character and role of Enobarbus.

The character of Antony's lieutenant Enobarbus contributes to the drama in a number of ways. Sympathetic to Antony from the start, his loyalty and fellow feeling help to establish the humanity of his captain in the course of the action. When at the beginning Antony says he wishes he had never met Cleopatra, instead of agreeing with him, he offers the rejoinder that, had that been the case, Antony would have missed, 'a wonderful / piece of work' (I.2.154–5). He does not share, therefore, the perspective of his fellow Roman soldiers Philo and Demetrius in the opening scene. In fact he is obviously enjoying life in Egypt and contributes to the relaxed humour of the Egyptian court, with appreciative comments, too, on Cleopatra.

When Antony says of Cleopatra, 'She is cunning past man's thought', Enobarbus disagrees: 'Alack, sir, no; her passions are made of / nothing but the finest part of pure love'(I.2.146–8). In their conversations at the beginning, and indeed in his role throughout, it is as if Enobarbus repre- sents an ordinary reflection of something in Antony himself, as in a mirror. His wit and humour in response to the announcement of Fulvia's death (though eventually Antony silences him with, 'No more light answers' (I.2.177)) anticipate the jovial side of Antony that will manifest itself in the galley scene.

Before the triumvirs meet, the diplomatic Lepidus tries to persuade Enobarbus to keep Antony calm and cool. Enobarbus will have none of it, saying he much prefers that Antony should speak his mind. He is forthright himself when he reminds Antony and Caesar that there will be time enough to quarrel after they have disposed of Pompey. To Antony's rebuke, 'Thou art a soldier only. Speak no more' (II.2.111), he boldly replies, 'That truth should be silent I had almost / forgot'. He is established here as a honest figure who gets to the heart of things and is not afraid to speak his mind.

His appreciation of Egypt and its queen, together with his wit and humour make him the perfect vehicle for the exotic description of Cleopatra given to his peers from Caesar's entourage. Coming as it does from him, this picture acquires a special authority. Though he is not a subtle politician, he is not without tact when he tries to stop Pompey making remarks to Antony about Julius Caesar's relations with Cleopatra. He then tells Pompey that he does not like him much but is prepared to give him his due. Pompey acknowledges his 'plainness' (II.6.78), his honesty in speaking.

In a witty exchange with Pompey's lieutenant Menas, he is loyal to Antony, but frankly says that, 'He will to his Egyptian dish again' (II.6.124) and predicts that the marriage to Octavia will prove a cause of friction between Caesar and Antony rather than a bond. He joins in the merry-making on board Pompey's galley, and mocks the hung-over Lepidus the morning after. Before Antony and Caesar come to blows, he is established as a truthful, honourable, witty and worldly fellow who is clear-sighted in his political and personal judgements.

When it comes to the conflict, he tries unsuccessfully to persuade Cleopatra not to be present personally in Antony's camp and he argues forcefully against the decision to fight by sea. He reports the flight of Cleopatra and after the naval disaster says that he will stay with Antony though it is against reason. His first thoughts of desertion, which he rejects, are prompted by Antony's self-betrayal, partially acknowledged by Antony himself when he says, 'I have fled myself' (III.11.7).When Cleopatra asks him who is to blame, he tells her directly that nobody forced Antony to follow when she flew; he is to blame.

In a series of asides, he comments on the folly of Antony's personal challenge to Caesar, on his own folly on following a fool, and makes sardonic comments on the response of first Cleopatra and then Antony in their dealings and treatment of Caesar's messenger. In a soliloquy – 'Now he'll outstare the lightning' (III.13.195–200) – he sees through Antony's bombastic rhetoric, implying that it is final evidence of the overthrow of all reason and he comes to his decision to leave Antony. He has clarified the meaning of the action and acts almost as an incarnation of Antony's reasonable self when this has departed from Antony; his departure coincides with Antony's loss of judgement.

After the assertion of reason, emotion comes to the fore in the final phase. As Antony addresses his servants as if for the last time, Enobarbus protests that he is 'onion-eyed' (IV.2.35); Antony is unmanning the troops. Antony's reaction to his desertion, 'O, my fortunes have / Corrupted honest men' (IV.5.16–7) and his decision to send his treasure to him confirm in the action of the play all that is said of Antony's 'bounty', which is otherwise only hearsay. The guilt felt by Enobarbus and his subsequent depression and loss of will are a counterpoint to the temporary and insecurely founded elation on Antony's side and are a product of the general disintegration that afflicts the affairs of Antony in the war with Caesar. But his death in mental torment and the consciousness of disgrace is proof of the fact that Antony's 'fortunes have corrupted honest men' and gives a wider dimension to the **tragedy** of the protagonists.

As well as being a reliable guide offering a perspective of common sense in both political and personal matters in a play of many shifts, moods and manoeuvres, his role is to be a kind of shadow attached to the larger figure of Antony. His fate proves to be indissolubly linked to his master. And the death of Enobarbus, unheroic but undeluded, is a counterpoint and prelude to what is to come. In the play's construction, his is not merely a supporting role, like those of Charmian and Iras; it is more intricately implicated in the general design; always a clarifying role, what it clarifies at the end is the tragic betrayal of honour in the world that is disintegrating around Antony.

LANGUAGE

The language of Shakespeare's plays, like the theatre for which they were written, contains a wide variety of elements from high to low. The language of *Antony and Cleopatra* shares stylistic features that are common in varying degrees to all Shakespeare's plays. For instance, Samuel Johnson memorably remarked on Shakespeare's fondness for wordplay: 'A quibble was to him the fatal Cleopatra for which he lost the world and was content to lose it' (Walter Raleigh, ed., *Johnson on Shakespeare*, OUP, 1908, p. 24). This talent for wordplay may unexpectedly transform the commonplace, as when the argumentative Cleopatra impudently asks Antony, 'Can Fulvia die?' (I.3.58). This single pun, playing on the secondary meaning of the word 'die' which refers in Elizabethan English to the sexual climax, might be said to represent in miniature the **tragicomic** vision of life embodied in so many of the plays. Wordplay in Shakespeare, like death, is a great leveller; even the straight-laced Caesar is not above a pun as he royally complains that in Antony's absence, 'we do bear / So great weight in his lightness' (I.4.24–5), lightness referring both to neglect of duty and levity.

There is, however, something distinctive about the language of this play to which reference has already been made in the notes. Its grand vision of things is created and sustained by its grand language. The use of **hyperbole**, the **figure of speech** which emphasises through exaggeration, is particularly pronounced in speeches made by Antony and Cleopatra and in speeches made about them. **Hyperbole** is apparent in the very first speech of the play. In describing Antony's 'dotage' that, 'O'erflows the measure' (I.1.2), Philo says Antony's heart which formerly in fights, 'hath burst / The buckles on his breast' (a somewhat heightened version of the truth) now, 'is become the bellows and the fan / To cool a gypsy's lust', where the action of the heart is again represented by an exaggerated **figure of speech** (I.1.7–10). Earlier 'his goodly eyes' were said to have 'glowed like plated Mars' (I.1.4), that is, like the war god in shining armour, where the grand **simile** has a heightening effect.

In an equally grand comparison, Cleopatra is likened to Venus. There are many mythological references which serve to put the characters in an exalted light which supports their own sense of their high status; Cleopatra is reported to have appeared, 'In thy habiliments of the goddess Isis' (III.6.17), the Egyptian goddess of the moon. References to the moon, the sun and the stars give a cosmic dimension to this **hyperbolic** style: 'Alack! Our terrene moon / Is now eclipsed, and it portends alone / The fall of Antony' (III.13.153–5). The grand note is further sustained in allusions to the elements, as in Cleopatra's declaration, 'I am fire and air; my other elements / I give to baser life' (V.2.288–9) and in the following **hyperbole**: 'I, that with my sword / Quartered the world, and o'er green Neptune's back / With ships made cities' (IV.14.57–9) or, 'His legs bestrid the ocean'

(V.2.82). All this is probably what led Samuel Coleridge (1772–1834), in a much repeated phrase, to speak of the 'happy valiancy' of the style in this play, its felicitous daring.

In addition to the use of **hyperbole** and the grand comparison which may be regarded as a complement to **hyperbole**, the language of the play is marked by the use of various figures of wit (the poetic intelligence), like **paradox** (an unexpected, apparently illogical or self contradictory statement), **oxymoron** (the union of opposites) and **conceit** (a far fetched comparison). Many of these figures are associated with Cleopatra and used to express her 'infinite variety' (see Textual Analysis). These figures of wit are often employed for comic purposes; for example, Enobarbus on hearing of the death of Fulvia likens the gods to the tailors of the earth in removing worn out robes and extends the **conceit** over several lines (I.2.162–71). But they are also to be found at moments of high seriousness, as when Antony declares to Eros, 'with a wound I must be cured' (IV.14.78), and after Eros has killed himself and Antony is about to fall on his sword, Antony plays on the idea of teaching and learning, invoking Eros with the words, 'Thy master dies thy scholar' (IV.14.102).

There are also recurrent patterns of imagery, some of which can be mentioned briefly here with one or two prominent examples. Food and drink are particularly, though not exclusively, associated with Egypt: 'Now no more / The juice of Egypt's grape shall moist this lip' (V.2.280–1). Egypt is a place of pleasure, but also of mystery and danger, encapsulated in the Nile imagery particularly involving the serpent. Cleopatra herself reports Antony addressing her as his 'serpent of old Nile' (I.5.25). Antony's sword is a material object, but it is also a recurring symbol of his military prowess and masculine identity. In a play in which the main characters are intensely conscious of their public status and of their grand self images – 'But since my lord / Is Antony again, I will be Cleopatra (III.13.185–6) – there are allusions to acting and the theatre. Cleopatra tauntingly bids Antony, 'play one scene / Of excellent dissembling' (I.3.78–9) and in her mind's eye sees, 'Some squeaking Cleopatra boy my greatness' (V.2.220). There is great irony and wit in this, given that the part of Cleopatra on the Jacobean stage, like all women's parts, would have been played by a boy.

Finally there is a complex of ideas associated with the word 'fortune', which can mean luck, success or perhaps fate, depending on the context. At the root of its use is the medieval image of the goddess Fortuna, the turning of whose wheel changes irreversibly the fortunes of her mortal underlings. The interpreter of fortune in Egypt is cryptic in his responses to Cleopatra's maids. In a pivotal scene, Antony asks the soothsayer whose fortunes shall rise higher, his or Caesar's. As a result of the reply he leaves Rome. After the first battle, 'Fortune and Antony part here' (IV.12.19). Caesar is 'full-fortuned' (IV.15.24) though as far as Cleopatra is concerned, 'Not being Fortune, he's but Fortune's knave' (V.2.3) and with Antony she mocks, 'The luck of Caesar'(V.2.285). In the general design this chain of imagery serves to give **unity** to the plot; it also has the effect of hinting at an inevitable destiny underlying the surface of the play's action and working through the decisions and errors and of the human participants.

PART FOUR

TEXTUAL ANALYSIS

TEXT 1

ACT II, SCENE 2, LINES 196–251

Antony, having returned to Rome to meet his fellow triumvirs to deal with the threat posed by Pompey, has just agreed to marry Octavia, Caesar's sister. The triumvirs have left the stage and Enobarbus is telling Maecenas and Agrippa, Caesar's followers, about life in Egypt. The subject soon turns to Cleopatra and her first meeting with Antony. This famous passage is based quite closely upon the description that Shakespeare read in North's Plutarch (see Further Reading). Comparison with North's prose will serve to throw into distinct relief certain characteristics of Shakespeare's poetic technique here and throughout the play.

(The italicised words mark material common to both North and Shakespeare. The passage in North can be found on pages 214–5 of The New Penguin Shakespeare.)

> ENOBARBUS
> The *barge* she sat in, like a burnished throne,
> Burned on the water. The *poop* was beaten *gold*;
> *Purple* the *sails*, and so perfumèd that
> The winds were lovesick with them. The *oars* were *silver*,
> Which to the tune of *flutes kept stroke*, and made
> The water which they beat to follow faster,
> As amorous of their strokes. For her own *person*,
> It beggared all description. She did lie
> In her *pavilion*, *cloth-of-gold* of *tissue*,
> O'erpicturing that *Venus* where we see
> The fancy outwork nature. On each side her
> Stood *pretty* dimpled *boys*, like smiling *cupids*,
> With divers-coloured *fans*, whose wind did seem
> To glow the delicate cheeks which they did cool,
> And what they undid did.

AGRIPPA   O, rare for Antony!

ENOBARBUS

Her *gentlewomen*, like the *Nereides*,
So many *mermaids*, tended her i'th'eyes,
And made their bends adornings. At the *helm*
A seeming mermaid steers. The silken *tackle*
Swell with the touches of those flower-soft hands,
That yarely frame the office. From the barge
A strange invisible *perfume* hits the sense
Of the adjacent *wharfs*. The city cast
Her people out upon her; and Antony,
Enthroned i'th'*market-place*, did sit *alone*,
Whistling to th'air; which, but for vacancy,
Had gone to gaze on Cleopatra too,
And made a gap in nature.

AGRIPPA   Rare Egyptian!

ENOBARBUS

Upon her landing, Antony *sent* to her,
Invited her to *supper*. She replied,
It should be better he became her guest;
Which she entreated. Our courteous Antony,
Whom ne'er the word of 'No' woman heard speak,
Being barbered ten times o'er, goes to the feast,
And, for his ordinary, pays his heart
For what his eyes eat only.

AGRIPPA   Royal wench!

She made great Caesar lay his sword to bed.
He ploughed her, and she cropped.

ENOBARBUS   I saw her once

Hop forty paces through the public street;
And, having lost her breath, she spoke, and panted,
That she did make defect perfection,
And, breathless, power breathe forth.

MAECENAS

Now Antony must leave her utterly.

ENOBARBUS

Never; he will not.
Age cannot wither her, nor custom stale
Her infinite variety. Other women cloy
The appetites they feed, but she makes hungry
Where most she satisfies; for vilest things
Become themselves in her, that the holy priests
Bless her, when she is riggish.

MAECENAS

If beauty, wisdom, modesty, can settle
The heart of Antony, Octavia is
A blessèd lottery to him.

AGRIPPA   Let us go.
Good Enobarbus, make yourself my guest
Whilst you abide here.

ENOBARBUS   Humbly, sir, I thank you.

Exeunt

And now North's text:

Therefore when she was sent unto by divers letters, both from Antonius himself and
also from his friends, she made so light of it and mocked Antonius so much that she
disdained to set forward otherwise but to take her *barge* on the river Cydnus, the *poop*
whereof was of *gold*, the *sails* of *purple*, and the *oars* of *silver*, which *kept stroke* in
rowing after the sound of the music of *flutes*, howboys, citherns, viols, and such other
instruments as they played upon in the barge. And now for the *person* of herself; she
was laid under a *pavilion of cloth-of-gold of tissue*, apparelled and attired like the
goddess *Venus* commonly drawn in *picture*; and hard by her, on either hand of her,
pretty fair *boys* apparelled as painters do set forth god *Cupid*, with little *fans* in their
hands, with the which they fanned *wind* upon her. Her ladies and *gentlewomen* also,
the fairest of them were apparelled like the nymphs *Nereides* (which are the *mermaids*
of the waters) and like the Graces, some steering the helm, others tending the *tackle*
and ropes of the *barge*, out of the which there came a wonderful passing sweet savour
of *perfumes*, that perfumed the *wharf's* side, pestered with innumerable multitudes of
people. Some of them followed the barge all alongst the river's side; others also ran
out of the city to see her coming in; so that in the end there ran such multitudes of

people come after another to see her that *Antonius* was left post-*alone in the market-place* in his imperial seat to give audience. And there went out a rumour in the people's mouths that the goddess Venus was come to play with the god Bacchus, for the general good of all Asia.

When Cleopatra *landed, Antonius sent to invite her to supper* to him. But she sent him word again, he should do *better* rather to come and sup with her. Antonius therefore, to show himself *courteous* unto her at her arrival, was contented to obey her, and went to supper with her; where he found such passing sumptuous fare, that no tongue can express it.

Quoted in T.B.L. Spencer, ed., *Shakespeare's Plutarch*, 1964, pp. 200–202

In the structure and order of his description and in the incidents described Shakespeare follows North closely. Many of the actual words used in the description are the same. North's description in itself is arresting and appeals strongly to the imagination. Yet in comparison with Shakespeare it seems prosaic, not merely because it is prose with a greater diffuseness but because it is so much less figurative. It is not true to say that North is not figurative at all. There are three striking **similes** at the heart of his description which together make the whole scene into an artistic tableau: Cleopatra is likened to Venus, the goddess of love, the pretty boys are like Cupid and her gentlewomen are like Nereides, sea nymphs, daughters of the sea god Nereus.

Shakespeare has retained North's basic conception, but has composed his tableau with greater artistry. In each of his versions of the three comparisons he has amplified North and gone one better. The first of these comparisons in which Cleopatra is likened to Venus provides the key to Shakespeare's method here, to the working of his imagination in this passage.

Cleopatra's person is imagined as 'o'erpicturing that Venus where we see / The fancy outwork nature'. Three orders of reality are implied here. There is nature, in the sense of beautiful women we know in the real world. Then there is art, through which the imagination of the artist, the 'fancy', is able to go one better by ironing out the imperfections of nature so that the beauty of the resulting picture perfects nature, giving us a classic Venus. Thirdly there is Cleopatra transcending even the classic Venus of the artist's imagination. Her beauty is thereby made to seem almost supernatural. This might be an absurd exaggeration if we had not already been prepared for something like this in the description that has gone before.

There are three striking figures, not mentioned in North, in the opening description. The barge, in a straightforward **simile**, is 'like a burnished throne', that is a gilt throne, suggesting majesty. But that it, 'Burned on the water' is a daring metaphor, **paradoxical** in its mingling of the opposing elements of water and fire. Secondly, the sails are so perfumed that the winds are 'lovesick' with them. Thirdly, the oars make the waves behind them follow faster, 'As amorous of their strokes', another striking metaphor. The winds and the waves are courting the barge. Shakespeare's imagination, his 'fancy', is working with the raw material of North and animating its elements with a series of poetic figures. This animation not only heightens the realism of North's prose, but also brings an erotic suggestiveness.

The strange beauty of the scene is mirrored in the action of the boys' fans, which have the **paradoxical** effect of seeming to make the cheeks glow which they are cooling. In glowing cheeks a gentle eroticism is delicately continued. Here Shakespeare has taken an imaginative idea from North (likening the boys to Cupids) amplified it and integrated it more closely into his overall vision of an exotic strangeness. The gentlewomen are described in terms that Shakespeare found in North. But once again the poet has integrated them into the scene much more effectively by making them subordinate to Cleopatra, describing how they watch every movement of her eyes and bow gracefully as they attend to her wishes. The queen's imperiousness is enhanced as she is the absolute centre of all attention.

Shakespeare also enhances the femininity of the scene in which the 'flower-soft hands' deftly handle the 'silken tackle'. The perfume is sweet in North, but more intriguingly strange in Shakespeare; its action as it, 'hits the sense / Of the adjacent wharfs' is much more arresting too. The whole passage, in fact, in both the prose and the poetry has a strong sensuous appeal, but Shakespeare manages to hit the senses by virtue both of stronger and of more subtle figurative suggestiveness.

With the rumour that Venus had come to play with Bacchus, the god of wine and revelry, for the good of all Asia, the description of Cleopatra's journey in North ends on a grand note. Shakespeare's very different conclusion, however, is both more daring and more fitting, given what has gone before and given the theme of his play. He follows North in having the city unpeopled and Antony left alone as everyone goes to see Cleopatra.

This is extravagance enough, but Shakespeare makes us imagine the impossible; the very air would have gone to gaze upon her if it could have done so without creating a vacancy in nature. This is another exaggeration that verges on the absurd but is not absurd because it grows naturally from the whole conception of the almost supernatural quality of Cleopatra's beauty and attractiveness. Like the wind and the water, the element of air pays court to the phenomenal beauty of the scene in which Cleopatra dominates, leaving poor Antony enthroned as befits his powerful status but, 'Whistling in th'air', rendered subjectless by the greater magnetism of the strange power of Cleopatra's attractiveness.

After the landing, we come down to earth, so to speak. The picture of Antony's courtesy and his elaborate grooming contain an element of humour; here Shakespeare has departed from North. In North the dinner is extravagant; Shakespeare makes a joke using the word 'ordinary' which is a public dinner but one that might be had in a tavern. The banquet itself is insignificant in comparison to what happens at it; Antony loses his heart, feasting his eyes on Cleopatra. By this stage Shakespeare has departed from his source.

Enobarbus follows with a less exotic description of Cleopatra hopping through the streets till she is breathless. In the scene as a whole it is something of a **paradox,** coming after the regal majesty of her presence and progress on her barge. It contains within itself a **paradox** when she is said to, 'make defect perfection'. What would be unbecoming in others is part of her completeness. This prepares us for the greater **paradoxes** of her 'infinite variety', where she is contrasted with other women in making hungry where most she satisfies: vile things in her are becoming and priests bless her when she is wanton.

The conception of her character therefore is grounded upon a **paradoxical** union of opposites. In itself this conception, which may be implicit in his source but is essentially Shakespeare's own, might not necessarily be convincing. What makes it convincing is the way that it is embodied and embedded in the language. The **paradoxes** are strongest at the end, but they are present in the extravagant language that evokes her mysterious beauty at the opening. The exaggerated language here, the use of **hyperbole,** is also present in the end: the idea that not just priests but holy priests, that is conscientious men of the cloth, bless her, whether literally or figuratively, when she is behaving like a harlot would be quite absurd if it was not wholly consistent with her spellbinding rarity, as established previously.

It would be wrong, however, to think of this scene solely as a more poetic version of the descriptive narrative account that we find in North's English version of Roman history. For this is drama and the dramatic dimension is crucial to its effect. Enobarbus has already been established in the audience's mind as a witty character who has a sharp-eyed appreciation of Cleopatra (I.2). The full **paradox** of his picture of the enchanting harlot queen is brought out in conversation with his fellow Romans.

The interventions of Agrippa do not merely break up what would otherwise be a very long account; they add an appreciative dimension and they propel it forward. Agrippa is a hardbitten Roman soldier; that he should respond to the magnetism of what he is hearing re-enacts its original effect upon Antony. Given that Egyptian was, in Shakespeare's day, synonymous with gypsy, there may be an **oxymoron** in 'Rare Egyptian!'. There certainly is an **oxymoron** in 'Royal wench', where wench is a word of low status with possible suggestions of lasciviousness.

There is a grand wordplay in Agrippa's line, 'She made great Caesar lay his sword to bed' (referring to Julius Caesar); this wittily reinforces the idea of Cleopatra's indomitable sexual power, for she has caused the most powerful man in the world to sheath his sword. That is, in political and military terms, not to kill or conquer her, and in sexual terms the sword can be understood to have obvious phallic associations in view of the ploughing and cropping of the next line (referring to sexual intercourse and the subsequent birth of Caesarion). This interjection has the effect of moving Enobarbus's account towards the more earthy aspects of Cleopatra. Indeed the whole scene is skilfully orchestrated, starting with the mysterious eroticism of the scene on the water, coming down to earth with the landing and descending finally to the word 'riggish'.

The intervention of Maecenas, towards the end of the scene, calls to mind the political imperative of the moment when he says that Antony must sever the link. After all that Enobarbus has said we are inclined to believe him when he says that Antony cannot do so. Finally when Maecenas hails the 'beauty, wisdom, modesty' of Octavia, starkly juxtaposed to the wantonness of Cleopatra, he evokes the alternative world that Antony has apparently embraced in agreeing to marry Octavia. Modesty is a well chosen word. In relations between the sexes it suggest chastity, in general behaviour it suggests humility, freedom from excess and self-control. Is it likely that Antony, who has been susceptible to Cleopatra and who has already shown evidence of passion and excess, can ever be content with the modest Octavia? This is the question with which we are left at the end.

The qualities of this extract are thrown into even clearer relief if it is juxtaposed with the description of the same journey put in the mouth of Antony by John Dryden (1631–1700) in his **neoclassical** play featuring Antony and Cleopatra, *All for Love or The World Well Lost* (1677).

ANTONY

Her galley down the silver Cydnos rowed,

The tackling silk, the streamers waved with gold;

The gentle winds were lodged in purple sails;

Her nymphs, like Nereids, round her couch were placed,

Where she, another sea-born Venus, lay.

DOLLABELLA

No more; I would not hear it.

ANTONY   Oh, you must!

She lay, and leant her cheek upon her hand,

And cast a look so languishingly sweet

As if, secure of all beholders' hearts,

Neglecting she could take 'em. Boys like Cupids

Stood fanning with their painted wings the winds

That played about her face; but if she smiled,

A darting glory seemed to blaze abroad,

That men's desiring eyes were never wearied,

But hung upon the object. To soft flutes

The silver oars kept time; and while they played,

The hearing gave new pleasure to the sight,

And both to thought. 'Twas Heaven, or somewhat more;

For so she charmed all hearts, that gazing crowds

Stood panting on the shore, and wanted breath

To give their welcome voice.

John Dryden, *All for Love*, New Mermaids, 1975, III. 162–82

The elements of North and his artistic tableau are still visible, but the supernatural strangeness and exotic appeal that we find in Shakespeare have evaporated along with all that created them: his **conceits, paradoxes** and daring **hyperboles**. Can we imagine Shakespeare's Cleopatra casting a look so languishingly sweet? That the sound of the flutes should provide food for 'thought' is a limiting response. In Shakespeare the picture hits the senses so that we are ravished beyond mere thinking about it. Dryden's verse is smooth and elegant (more so than Shakespeare's), but the effect is tame.

TEXT 2

ACT II, SCENE 5, LINES 1–66

After the triumvirs have settled their differences and Antony has agreed to marry Octavia, they depart. The scene now shifts to Alexandria, by which time Antony has made the marriage, unbeknown to Cleopatra.

CLEOPATRA
Give me some music – music, moody food
Of us that trade in love.

ALL   The music, ho!

Enter Mardian the Eunuch

CLEOPATRA
Let it alone! Let's to billiards. Come, Charmian.

CHARMIAN
My arm is sore; best play with Mardian.

CLEOPATRA
As well a woman with an eunuch played
As with a woman. Come, you'll play with me, sir?

MARDIAN
As well as I can, madam.

CLEOPATRA
And when good will is showed, though't come too short,
The actor may plead pardon. I'll none now.
Give me mine angle. We'll to th'river; there,
My music playing far off, I will betray

Tawny-finned fishes. My bended hook shall pierce
Their slimy jaws; and as I draw them up,
I'll think them every one an Antony,
And say 'Ah, ha! Y'are caught!'

CHARMIAN   'Twas merry when
You wagered on your angling; when your diver
Did hang a salt fish on his hook, which he
With fervency drew up.

CLEOPATRA   That time – O times! –
I laughed him out of patience; and that night
I laughed him into patience; and next morn,
Ere the ninth hour, I drunk him to his bed;
Then put my tires and mantles on him, whilst
I wore his sword Philippan.

                    Enter a Messenger
                              O, from Italy!
Ram thou thy fruitful tidings in mine ears,
That long time have been barren.

MESSENGER   Madam, madam –

CLEOPATRA
Antonio's dead! If thou say so, villain,
Thou kill'st thy mistress; but well and free,
If thou so yield him, there is gold and here
My bluest veins to kiss, a hand that kings
Have lipped, and trembled kissing.

MESSENGER
First, madam, he is well.

CLEOPATRA   Why, there's more gold.
But, sirrah, mark, we use
To say the dead are well. Bring it to that,
The gold I give thee will melt and pour
Down thy ill-uttering throat.

MESSENGER
Good madam, hear me.

CLEOPATRA   Well, go to, I will.
But there's no goodness in thy face, if Antony
Be free and healthful; so tart a favour
To trumpet such good tidings? If not well,
Thou shouldst come like a Fury crowned with snakes,
Not like a formal man.

MESSENGER   Will't please you hear me?

CLEOPATRA
I have a mind to strike thee ere thou speak'st.
Yet, if thou say Antony lives, is well,
Or friends with Caesar, or not captive to him,
I'll set thee in a shower of gold, and hail
Rich pearls upon thee.

MESSENGER   Madam, he's well.

CLEOPATRA   Well said.

MESSENGER
And friends with Caesar.

CLEOPATRA   Th'art an honest man.

MESSENGER
Caesar and he are greater friends than ever.

CLEOPATRA
Make thee a fortune from me.

MESSENGER   But yet, madam –

CLEOPATRA
I do not like 'But yet'; it does allay
The good precedence. Fie upon 'But yet'!
'But yet' is as a gaoler to bring forth
Some monstrous malefactor. Prithee, friend,
Pour out the pack of matter to mine ear,
The good and bad together. He's friends with Caesar,
In state of health, thou sayst, and, thou sayst, free.

MESSENGER
Free, madam! No; I made no such report.
He's bound unto Octavia.

CLEOPATRA   For what good turn?

MESSENGER
For the best turn i'th'bed.

CLEOPATRA   I am pale, Charmian.

MESSENGER
Madam, he's married to Octavia.

CLEOPATRA
The most infectious pestilence upon thee!

She strikes him down

MESSENGER
Good madam, patience.

CLEOPATRA   What say you?

She strikes him

                 Hence,
Horrible villain, or I'll spurn thine eyes
Like balls before me! I'll unhair thy head!

She hales him up and down

Thou shalt be whipped with wire and stewed in brine,
Smarting in lingering pickle!

Though striking messengers is doubtless highly reprehensible behaviour (and drawing a knife on them, as Cleopatra does at the end of this scene, certainly is), this is a richly comic scene and a welcome change after the political manoeuvring in Rome. At the opening, missing Antony, Cleopatra is bored. Although we are always conscious of her regal status, we never see her engaged in matters of serious statecraft in the first part of the drama. Egypt is here the playful setting for music, games, sex talk and mirth.

    To begin with the humour is at the expense of Mardian, the eunuch. There is bawdy innuendo, in which Mardian himself takes part, on the eunuch's inability to play properly with a woman sexually. Playing with Mardian then ceases to be an attractive proposition. Cleopatra's whim turns towards fishing. The humour now is at the expense of Antony. She will imagine every fish she catches to be Antony. The imagery here supports the notion that Antony is wholly entangled by the wily Cleopatra, who has her hooks in him, so to speak. Charmian reminds her of the time she played a trick on Antony by fixing a salted fish to his line which he then drew in with verve and enthusiasm as if it had been his own catch. Once again, Cleopatra is dominant, mocking and playing tricks upon her lover. More tricks follow when she recalls dressing him up in her clothes, while she wears his 'sword Philippan'. In this reversal of the usual roles, which had so scandalised Caesar when he heard report of it (I.4.5–7), she is again the dominant party, symbolically usurping the masculine role.

The messenger enters with what the audience knows will be bad news for Cleopatra. Shakespeare uses dramatic irony here, exploiting the audience's superior knowledge for comic effect. He spins the scene out by making it difficult for the poor messenger to get a word in edgeways. Cleopatra's opening – a forceful sexual innuendo – is quite startling: 'Ram thou thy fruitful tidings in mine ears, / That long time have been barren.' The normal social inhibitions do not apply to Cleopatra.

Her grand extravagance is apparent in the melodrama of her first speech. In it she imagines the messenger announcing Antony's death and then, if he pronounces him well, promises gold and her, 'bluest veins to kiss' – emphasising her blue-blooded regality – 'a hand that kings / Have lipped, and trembled kissing'. She is revealed here in full confidence of her sexual power. The punishment she envisages for him (melting the gold and pouring it down his throat) if still he should pronounce him dead, is correspondingly extreme and grand, as are the images of the Fury, the shower of gold and the hail of pearls. Shakespeare has endowed her with a rich and fertile imagination. (Crassus, a member of the First Triumvirate, died at the hands of the Parthians by having molten gold poured into his mouth. A brutally ironic death, it reflected the Parthian view that he had come simply to steal their gold (see Chronology).)

The scene builds up tension and then releases it in a highly effective dramatic explosion. Cleopatra's long comment on 'But yet' which she rightly sees as, 'a gaoler to bring forth / Some monstrous malefactor' prepares us and her for the worst. Her misunderstanding of the messenger's meaning in 'bound' resulting in his joke 'the best turn i'th'bed' intensifies the irony. When finally the messenger delivers his news simply and directly in one line, the suspense that has been mounting is finally over. Cleopatra's sudden invective matches in verbal terms her physical action and in its extremity befits her tempestuous character. The scene exhibits her dominance and shows her to be driven by strong and uncontrollable passions. It also shows us what Enobarbus has described in his picture of her: a character of apparent contradictions, queen, virago and fishwife, all somehow cohering in one linguistic creation.

TEXT 3

ACT IV, SCENE 15, LINES 13–90

After Antony's bungled attempt at suicide, a messenger informs him that Cleopatra, whom he believed to have committed suicide, is still alive and has taken refuge in her monument. He gives orders that he be taken to her.

CLEOPATRA
Help, friends below! Let's draw him hither.

ANTONY   Peace!
Not Caesar's valour hath o'erthrown Antony,
But Antony's hath triumphed on itself.

CLEOPATRA
So it should be, that none but Antony
Should conquer Antony, but woe 'tis so!

ANTONY
I am dying, Egypt, dying; only
I here importune death awhile, until
Of many thousand kisses the poor last
I lay upon thy lips.

CLEOPATRA   I dare not, dear;
Dear my lord, pardon. I dare not,
Lest I be taken. Not th'imperious show
Of the full-fortuned Caesar ever shall
Be brooched with me. If knife, drugs, serpents, have
Edge, sting, or operation, I am safe.
Your wife Octavia, with her modest eyes

And still conclusion, shall acquire no honour
Demuring upon me. But come, come, Antony –
Help me, my women – we must draw thee up.
Assist, good friends.

ANTONY   O, quick, or I am gone.

CLEOPATRA
Here's sport indeed! How heavy weighs my lord!
Our strength is all gone into heaviness,
That makes the weight. Had I great Juno's power,
The strong-winged Mercury should fetch thee up
And set thee by Jove's side. Yet come a little;
Wishers were ever fools, O, come, come, come.

They heave Antony aloft to Cleopatra
And welcome, welcome! Die when thou hast lived;
Quicken with kissing. Had my lips that power,
Thus would I wear them out.

ALL THE GUARDS   A heavy sight!

ANTONY
I am dying, Egypt, dying.
Give me some wine, and let me speak a little.

CLEOPATRA
No, let me speak, and let me rail so high
That the false housewife Fortune break her wheel,
Provoked by my offence.

ANTONY   One word, sweet queen.
Of Caesar seek your honour, with your safety. O!

CLEOPATRA
They do not go together.

ANTONY   Gentle, hear me:
None about Caesar trust but Proculeius.

CLEOPATRA
My resolution and my hands I'll trust,
None about Caesar.

ANTONY

The miserable change now at my end
Lament nor sorrow at, but please your thoughts
In feeding them with those my former fortunes
Wherein I lived; the greatest prince o'th'world,
The noblest; and do now not basely die,
Not cowardly put off my helmet to
My countryman; a Roman, by a Roman
Valiantly vanquished. Now my spirit is going;
I can no more.

CLEOPATRA　　Noblest of men, woo't die?
Hast thou no care of me? Shall I abide
In this dull world, which in thy absence is
No better than a sty? O, see, my women,

Antony dies

The crown o'th'earth doth melt. My lord!
O, withered is the garland of the war,
The soldier's pole is fall'n; young boys and girls
Are level now with men. The odds is gone,
And there is nothing left remarkable
Beneath the visiting moon.

She faints

CHARMIAN　　　　　　　　　O, quietness, lady!

IRAS

She's dead too, our sovereign.

CHARMIAN　　　　　　　　　Lady!

IRAS　　　　　　　　　　　　Madam!

CHARMIAN

O madam, madam, madam!

IRAS

Royal Egypt! Empress!

CHARMIAN　　　　　　　　Peace, peace, Iras!

CLEOPATRA

No more but e'en a woman, and commanded
By such poor passion as the maid that milks
And does the meanest chares. It were for me
To throw my sceptre at the injurious gods,
To tell them that this world did equal theirs
Till they had stolen our jewel. All's but naught.
Patience is sottish, and impatience does
Become a dog that's mad; then is it sin,
To rush into the secret house of death
Ere death dare come to us? How do you, women?
What, what, good cheer! Why, how now, Charmian?
My noble girls! Ah, women, women, look,
Our lamp is spent, it's out. Good sirs, take heart.
We'll bury him; and then, what's brave, what's noble,
Let's do't after the high Roman fashion,
And make death proud to take us. Come, away.
This case of that huge spirit now is cold.
Ah, women, women! Come; we have no friend
But resolution, and the briefest end.

Exeunt, bearing off Antony's body

In Antony's death scene, the presentation of the lovers confirms and consolidates the impression they have made throughout the play. What is new in the case of Antony is a touching concern for Cleopatra's safety and honour. Coming from the battlefield where he has just been defeated, although he desires to kiss her a final time, his thoughts are almost entirely upon his own honour and reputation as a soldier. In a formal speech, he asks to be remembered for his former glory, concluding with the dignified assertion that he is, 'a Roman, by a Roman / Valiantly vanquished'.

It may be that he has in mind his defeat by Caesar. Perhaps it is more likely, given his earlier comment to Cleopatra that: 'Not Caesar's valour hath o'erthrown Antony, / But Antony's hath triumphed on itself', that he is referring to the act of taking his own life. In the Roman world suicide was regarded as a noble act, as Cleopatra recognises at the end of the scene when she herself contemplates doing, 'what's brave, what's noble ... after the high Roman fashion'. But in either meaning, though it is a noble

·phrase, it does not quite ring true; after his botched suicide and all that has led up to it, Antony is putting on a brave face and the best gloss possible on what is a sorry state of affairs.

Until Antony has actually died, Cleopatra's thoughts too are primarily on her own safety and honour. She will not risk coming down to him; he has to be brought up to her. (Some commentators have seen an echo here of the scene in which Cleopatra envisages drawing up Antony on a fish-hook.) Prominent in her mind is the thought that she might become an ornament ('Be brooched') in the triumphal spectacle ('th'imperious show') of the successful Caesar, where Octavia may gain 'honour', that is reputation and status, by an intolerable exercise of virtue at her expense. Far from being absorbed in each other to the exclusion of all else, therefore, the lovers exhibit the intense self-regard that they have shown from the beginning.

Antony's sense of himself as a valiant, indeed triumphant, Roman is matched by the regal imperiousness of Cleopatra, reflected in many of the words and images used by her and those about her. She is sovereign – 'Royal Egypt' – and empress; she talks of a crown, her sceptre and a jewel. She associates herself with divinity when she wishes she had Juno's power to set Antony by Jove. Her grand extravagance is reflected in characteristic **hyperboles**: she would rail so strongly that Fortune might break her wheel, she would find it becoming to throw her sceptre against the gods that permit this harm and hurt.

Yet the imperial note is only one of several sounded in her language in this scene: there is ironic awareness in, 'Here's sport indeed!' and in the wordplay on 'weighs' that follows, meaning both physical weight and the weight of grief, her smart verbal intelligence is harnessed to pathetic effect. Her sensuality, too, is evoked when she welcomes Antony with kisses, even if they cannot quicken him into life. Some commentators have seen sexual meaning in her use of the words die and quicken here. If it is there, far from being unfitting, it maintains the consistency of her characterisation.

Before this extract Antony has been on stage for some time and we have been absorbed in his fate. But it is characteristic of the pattern of their relationship as Shakespeare has presented it that even his death should be upstaged by Cleopatra. As soon as Antony has died she takes centre stage and dominates the remainder of the play. Just as her real feelings for Antony are first seen after he has departed from Egypt ('O happy horse, to bear the weight of Antony!' I.5.21), so at the moment of his departure they come to the surface here. What is most moving is the **paradox** that her words both sustain the image of Antony as a powerful military hero ('O, withered is the garland of the war') while at the same time recognising that death obliterates all the distinctions by which they have lived their lives ('young boys and girls / Are level now with men').

After she has fainted, in what is perhaps her most human and moving moment in the play, she sees that this levelling effect applies to herself too: 'No more but e'en a woman'. Where Antony had been restrained and formal in his acceptance of the inevitable at the end, Cleopatra's final speech is characteristically varied in its emotional range and fluid in its movement. She humbly identifies with 'the maid that milks' at the beginning then grandly with the gods themselves whom she deigns to upbraid. She shifts again, in feeling that patience is for fools while to rail is madness. As her thoughts turn to death, they also look beyond herself to her maidservants. After the shifts and swings in mood and thought (what an opportunity for an accomplished actress), as she contemplates a way to, 'make death proud to take us' she reasserts her wavering sense of identity in the calm resolution (both courage and decision) of the close.

PART FIVE

Background

William Shakespeare

There are no personal records of Shakespeare's life. Official documents and occasional references to him enable us to draw the main outline of his public life, but his private life remains hidden. What we do know can be quickly summarised.

Shakespeare was born into a well-to-do family in the market town of Stratford-upon-Avon in Warwickshire, where he was baptised, in Holy Trinity Church, on 26 April 1564. His father, John Shakespeare, was a prosperous glover and leather merchant who became a person of some importance in the town: in 1565 he was elected an alderman of the town, and in 1568 he became high bailiff (or mayor) of Stratford. In 1557 he had married Mary Arden. Their third child (of eight) and eldest son, William, learned to read and write at the primary (or 'petty') school in Stratford and then, it seems probable, attended the local grammar school, where he would have studied Latin, history, logic and rhetoric. In November 1582 William, then aged eighteen, married Anne Hathaway, who was twenty-six years old. They had a daughter, Susanna, in May 1583, and twins, Hamnet and Judith, in 1585.

Shakespeare next appears in the historical record in 1592 when he was mentioned as a London actor and playwright in a pamphlet by the dramatist Robert Greene. During the next twenty years, he continued to live in London, regularly visiting his wife and family in Stratford. He continued to act, but his chief fame was as a dramatist. From 1594 he wrote exclusively for the Lord Chamberlain's Men, which rapidly became the leading dramatic company and from 1603 enjoyed the patronage of James I as the King's Men. His plays were extremely popular and he became a shareholder in the theatre company. He was able to buy lands around Stratford and a large house in the town, to which he retired about 1611. He died there on April 23 1616 and was buried in Holy Trinity Church on 25 April.

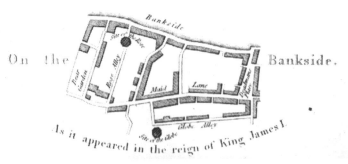

THE GLOBE THEATRE,

On the Bankside.

As it appeared in the reign of King James I.

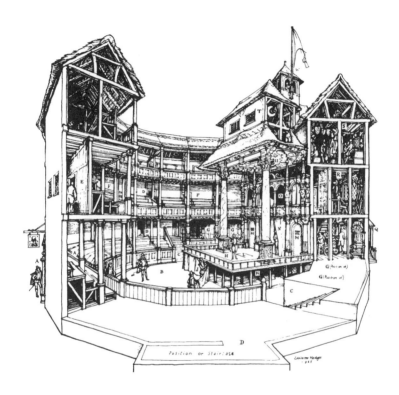

A CONJECTURAL RECONSTRUCTION OF THE INTERIOR OF THE GLOBE PLAYHOUSE

AA Main entrance
B   The Yard
CC Entrances to lowest galleries
D   Entrance to staircase and upper galleries
E   Corridor serving the different sections of the
    middle gallery
F   Middle gallery ('Twopenny Rooms')
G   'Gentlemen's Rooms or Lords Rooms'
H   The stage
J   The hanging being put up round the stage
K   The 'Hell' under the stage
L   The stage trap, leading down to the Hell
MM Stage doors

N   Curtained 'place behind the stage'
O   Gallery above the stage, used as required
    sometimes by musicians, sometimes
    by spectators, and often as part of the
    play
P   Back-stage area (the tiring-house)
Q   Tiring-house door
R   Dressing-rooms
S   Wardrobe and storage
T   The hut housing the machine for lowering
    enthroned gods, etc., to the stage
U   The 'Heavens'
W   Hoisting the playhouse flag

Between the late 1580s and 1613 Shakespeare wrote thirty-seven plays and contributed to some by other dramatists. An exact chronology of the plays is not possible; the dates below give the earliest and latest dates for their writing and performance.

He began by rewriting earlier plays and working plotlines inspired by the classics. *The Comedy of Errors* (1590–4), for example, is based upon *The Brothers Menaechmi* by the Roman playwright Plautus. Among his earlier plays, which are comedies and histories for the most part, is his **tragedy** of young love *Romeo and Juliet* (1591–7), which makes an interesting comparison with the later *Antony and Cleopatra* (1606–8) written in middle age and featuring middle-aged lovers. His English history plays, completed with *Henry V* in 1599, tell an epic story which examines how modern England came into being through the conflicts of the fifteenth-century Wars of the Roses (from the emblems of the two factions of the British Royal family, the white rose of York and the red rose of Lancaster) which brought the Tudors to the throne. The two parts of *Henry IV* (1596–8), in which Falstaff, one of his most popular comic characters, appears, like *Antony and Cleopatra*, have a mixture of comic and serious scenes and public and private worlds.

The fascination he shows for the related subjects of politics and the exercise of power is manifest in his first major Roman play *Julius Caesar* (1598–1600). It is one of the advantages of the Roman setting that, in an age when plays were censored, this fascination can be pursued with a freedom and a detachment not possible in representing contemporary events or recent history.

As the new century begins a new note is detectable. Plays such as *Troilus and Cressida* (1601–2) and *Measure for Measure* (1603–4), poised between comedy and **tragedy**, evoke complex responses. Because of their generic uncertainty and ambivalent tone such works are sometimes referred to as 'problem plays'. *Antony and Cleopatra* has occasionally been set alongside these for comparison, though it is more usually discussed, together with the third great Roman play *Coriolanus* (1605–10), in comparison with the four great tragedies which it immediately follows: *Hamlet* (1600–1), *Othello* (1602–4), *King Lear* (1605–6) and *Macbeth* (1605–6). These six plays constitute Shakespeare's tragic period. *Antony and Cleopatra*, as a **tragedy** of love, may be fruitfully juxtaposed with *Othello*. These two plays and *Coriolanus* all feature great military heroes who come to grief through an inability to manage the personal and emotional side of their lives. His last plays, often called the late romances, do not have tragic resolutions; they end harmoniously in forgiveness and reconciliation.

HISTORICAL BACKGROUND

Shakespeare's early career is part of the great flowering in literature and culture that occurred in the late Elizabethan age, given impetus by the growth in national self-confidence resulting from the defeat of the Spanish Armada in 1588. This flowering is itself part of a wider movement rejuvenating European culture, which since the nineteenth century has been known by the term *Renaissance*. Meaning literally 'rebirth' it denotes a revival and redirection of artistic and intellectual endeavour which began in Italy in the fourteenth century in the poetry of Petrarch (1304–74). It spread gradually northwards across Europe, and is first detectable in England in the early sixteenth century in the writings of the scholar and statesman Sir Thomas More (1478–1535) and in the poetry of Sir Thomas Wyatt (1503–42) and Henry Howard, Earl of Surrey (c.1517–47), all associated with the court of Henry VIII. Its keynote was a curiosity in thought which challenged old assumptions and traditions. To the innovative spirit of the Renaissance, the preceding ages appeared dully unoriginal and conformist.

That spirit was fuelled by the rediscovery of many classical texts and the culture of Greece and Rome. This fostered a confidence in human reason and in human potential which, in every sphere, challenged old convictions. The discovery of America and its peoples (Columbus had sailed in 1492) demonstrated that the world was a larger and stranger place than had hitherto been thought. The cosmological speculation of Copernicus (1473–1543, later confirmed by Galileo, 1564–1642) that the sun, not the earth, was the centre of our planetary system challenged the centuries-old belief that the earth and human beings were at the centre of the cosmos. The pragmatic political philosophy of Machiavelli (1469–1527) seemed to cut politics free from its traditional link with morality by permitting statesmen any means which secured the desired end. And the religious movements we know collectively as the Reformation broke with the Church of Rome and set the individual conscience, not ecclesiastical authority, at the centre of the religious life. Nothing, it seemed, was beyond questioning, nothing impossible.

Shakespeare's drama is innovative and challenging in exactly the way of the Renaissance. It interrogates (examines and asks questions of) the beliefs, assumptions and politics upon which Elizabethan society was founded. And though the plays always conclude in a restoration of order and stability, many critics are inclined to argue that their imaginative energy goes into subverting, rather than reinforcing, traditional values.

LITERARY BACKGROUND

The positive legacy of the revival of the classics in the Renaissance was the critical spirit it fostered. Less positive was the preoccupation among neoclassicists with classical form. The breathtaking sweep of Shakespeare's imaginative treatment of the story of Antony and Cleopatra can be appreciated if his play is compared with an earlier version of the same material from Plutarch by the classically minded Samuel Daniel (1562–1619) in his closet drama *The Tragedie of Cleopatra* (1594). This was written in the form of a play but not intended for performance. Revised editions were published in 1599 and 1607. The whole play covers the events contained in Act V of Shakespeare's play. It has a moralising chorus, and Cleopatra feels guilty and complains at great length about past failings and present misfortunes. There is some psychological complexity but the action is comparatively static; even her death is narrated by a messenger.

Shakespeare may also have known the translation of Robert Garnier's tragedy *Marc Antoine* (1578). This was made by the countess of Pembroke and, her version *Antonius*, was printed in 1592 and 1595. The constraints of the **neoclassical** idea of a play prevented these sixteenth-century dramatists dramatising the love story from a point of view that embraced both lovers in a single vision.

Shakespeare may have composed his play with a famous classical treatment of the clash between love and Roman duty in his mind. The Latin epic poem of the Roman poet Virgil, *The Aeneid*, was published after his death in 19BC, a mere thirteen years after the battle of Actium. In it, the hero Aeneas, whose mission is to lead his Trojans after the fall of Troy to a new god-given destiny in Italy, encounters Dido, queen of Carthage, when he is shipwrecked on the African coast. He falls in love with her and has to be reminded by the gods of his mission. He then does the Roman thing and leaves for Italy to found the city in Latium that is to be the parent city of Rome itself.

Virgil's first readers must have seen reflected in this myth the recent historical events involving Antony and Cleopatra, and seen in Aeneas a character who, unlike Antony, puts his public duty before his personal inclinations. The dying Antony imagines himself and Cleopatra displacing Dido and Aeneas in the underworld presumably as the most famous lovers in the world (IV.14.53). This is an intriguing allusion. When Aeneas visited Dido in the underworld she refused to forgive him so that they were forever estranged. Many from Shakespeare's more learned audience would have known this. Like the play itself, Shakespeare's relation with his sources is often problematic.

PART SIX

CRITICAL HISTORY

EARLY RESPONSES

There is no evidence that *Antony and Cleopatra* was revived in the seventeenth century after its first performance; indeed in the absence of any precise record some scholars have doubted whether it was actually performed in Shakespeare's lifetime. Nor is there much evidence that, unlike other plays of Shakespeare such as *Hamlet*, it was part of the common stock of the educated person's reading and repertoire. Dryden had written his version of the story of Antony and Cleopatra in 1677, the simplicity of which is reflected in his title *All for Love or The World Well Lost* (this gives Shakespeare's more ambiguous play a definite 'romantic' slant). From this point the history of the two plays was intertwined for the next one hundred and fifty years. Dryden's play, which obeyed the **unities** of time, place and action, was more in accord with the dramatic theory and practice of what is sometimes called the **neoclassical** period extending from the second half of seventeenth century to the end of the eighteenth. In this period it was revived several times.

The first revival of Shakespeare's play came in 1759 and was mounted by the famous actor manager David Garrick. However it was not reproduced intact and there were many scenic rearrangements with Shakespeare's forty-two scenes being reduced to twenty-seven. Changes in location were restricted, some characters and many of the bawdy lines were excised. The political element was played down to give the love affair greater prominence. It was not a success.

Dryden continued to be revived well into the nineteenth century. In 1813 there was a production that amalgamated features from both Dryden and Shakespeare. It was not until 1849 that Samuel Phelps successfully mounted a sumptuous production of Shakespeare's play, though not without considerable cutting and scenic rearrangement, which finally supplanted Dryden's. The realistic style of nineteenth-century production, in which costumes and sets were researched with an archaeological precision, was very different from the spare style of the Elizabethan theatre where there was little scenery and where costumes were contemporary. This made it virtually impossible to reproduce Shakespeare's text with its great variety of scenes changes without quite major adjustment. It was not until this style was abandoned in the 1920s that the Shakespeare text that we know was deemed suitable for continuous performance. There is a vindication of the play's construction for stage performance by Harley Granville-Barker in his *Prefaces to Shakespeare* (1930).

Despite the lateness of its revival in the theatre, there is evidence to suggest that after the **neoclassical** period had ended (when the play's irregularity in breaking the **unities** and mixing the genres was a stumbling block to its appreciation), the play was highly thought of in the nineteenth century. William Hazlitt in *The Characters of Shakespeare's Plays* (1817) writes lyrically of the character of Cleopatra. The romantic poet Coleridge praised its poetry and asked whether it might rank alongside the four great **tragedies** which had immediately preceded it, *Hamlet* (1600–1), *Othello* (1602–4), *King Lear* (1605–6) and *Macbeth* (1605–6). This question was taken up by A.C. Bradley in 'Shakespeare's *Antony and Cleopatra*' published in *Oxford Lectures in Poetry* (1909). Remarking on the sparse dramatic action, the lack of an inner struggle evident in Antony as he leaves first Cleopatra and then Octavia, the spirit of irony that pervades the political aspects of the play, a lack of awareness in Cleopatra that she has destroyed Antony, and the theatrical self-awareness of the protagonists, particularly Cleopatra, he gives the answer no; for all its magnificence the play does not engage its audience as do the earlier **tragedies**.

The traditional tendency of earlier criticism to emphasise the transcendent vision of ennobling love, perhaps reaching its height in G. Wilson Knight's *The Imperial Theme* (1931), has led to a reaction that is more sceptical; on the one hand there are those like H. A. Mason, in *Shakespeare's Tragedies of Love* (1970), who see a weakness in the dramatic exploration of the play's theme which is not compensated for by the poetry, on the other, those who find its uncertainties and ambiguities deliberate, stressing the double view the play offers of its protagonists in love and politics, such as Janet Adelman in *The Common Liar* (1973).

As a play that deals with central issues of sexuality and power, *Antony and Cleopatra* continues to generate new analyses prompted by the new ways of looking at texts and analysing them that have become common in literary studies in recent years. In general it may be said that there has been a greater emphasis on political aspects of the play and in the wake of feminist criticism much interest in the issues of gender raised by the representation of the masculine and feminine in the play.

The tendency to regard Shakespeare's plays as transcending their time – perhaps most marked in the case of the Roman plays which do not have any immediately perceived connection with the British scene – has been subject to a variety of challenges in recent accounts. In *Radical Tragedy* (1984), Jonathan Dollimore argues that the plays represent on the stage a radical questioning of the traditional forms of authority in Church and State; this questioning or interrogation may be related to the later collapse of these traditional forms resulting in the Civil War that began in the reign of Charles I. In the case of *Antony and Cleopatra*, he argues that the conflict between Antony and Caesar represents a collision between older conceptions of power centred upon individual honour (associated with the old aristocracy) and a new conception of civil power in which personal honour is no longer the dominant factor. Antony is caught between the two. His relationship with Cleopatra is a kind of power play, reflecting the larger play of political power. Antony's love turns out to be a compensation for the loss of power. Far from being transcendent, the love affair is determined by relations of power.

A more specific account of the play's relation to history is to be found in 'Jacobean *Antony and Cleopatra*' (1985) where H. Neville Davies argues that the play had an immediate historical parallel in Jacobean court politics with James I representing himself as the British Augustus (Octavius Caesar took the name Augustus after his return from the east) maintaining peace in a united kingdom. The action of the play records the movement from triumvirate to universal monarchy; Caesar prophesies that, 'The time of universal peace is near' (IV.6.5). On this reading, since the play shows Caesar in an unflattering light, it can be regarded as sceptical and unsupportive of these claims of Jacobean propaganda.

In the general debate about issues of gender that has been stimulated by the feminist movement, particular interest has focused on whether there is an essential difference between male and female (other than obvious biological difference) or whether gender roles are socially constructed. This has stimulated greater awareness of the representation of masculine and feminine in the play. Traditional 'Roman' ideas of masculinity represented by Caesar (see especially his speech denouncing Antony for subverting the traditional masculine role at I.4.1ff and the confirmation of this in what Cleopatra says at II.5.22–3) may be seen to be threatened by Egyptian feminisation; alternatively Antony may represent a new more androgynous masculinity. Equally there is a debate about the extent to which Cleopatra might simply be an exotic version of the old stereotypes or whether she represents a powerful and positive new image for women (and men).

In a polemical essay, 'Egyptian Queens and Male Reviewers: Sexist Attitudes in *Antony and Cleopatra* Criticism' (1977), Linda T. Fitz takes issue with what she sees as the alternative views of traditional (man-made and male oriented) criticism: either Antony is destroyed in his 'dotage' by a treacherous strumpet, or the play celebrates a transcendent love, both views precluding a reasonable assessment of Cleopatra. She argues that many male critics feel personally threatened by the powerful Egyptian, revealing deep fears of aggressive or manipulative women. Equally, the fascination with her mysterious inscrutability can be seen as masking the common male view that all women are unfathomable (and probably irrational and whimsical). She argues that Cleopatra needs to be demystified and that her variety is finite. She laments the unwillingness of male critics to consider Cleopatra as a tragic protagonist on a level with Antony.

The character of Cleopatra raises questions not only about the representation of women but, since she is conceived as 'tawny fronted', of black women too. It is interesting to reflect that the Mediterranean Romans would probably not have attached much significance to the skin colour of a woman descended from Ptolemy (one of the generals of Alexander the Great who inherited the Egyptian part of his empire) who was actually of Greek origin. Differences with Cleopatra and Egypt for the Romans were more than skin deep; they rested on questions of politics and economics (the corn supply) rather than culture or race. Nevertheless in Plutarch as in Shakespeare Cleopatra is a representative of a culture that has values not usually associated with the Romans. The difference is there in Shakespeare, though it is not as accentuated as it could have been or as some commentators maintain. Cleopatra appears, 'In th'habiliments of the goddess Isis' (III.6.17) when she is formally endowed with kingdoms by

Antony (here the affront is political; from Caesar's point of view Antony had no business creating a power centre to rival Rome). She nevertheless speaks in the language of the Graeco-Roman tradition; her gods and heroes, Hercules, Mars, Juno, Mercury and Jove are those of Greece and Rome.

In the wake of Edward Said's *Orientalism* (Routledge & Kegan Paul, 1978), the representation of Cleopatra, alluring, magnificent, enchanting and exotic, has been seen as a typical western mystification of the oriental; a figment of the imagination that fails to be credible when viewed from a non-western perspective. In post-imperial times, too, Cleopatra in her relations with the Romans is seen to be fighting Roman imperialism; indeed, in history, after her suicide, Caesar annexed Egypt for the empire and it became a Roman province.

PART SEVEN

Broader perspectives

Further reading

Shakespeare's sources for antony and cleopatra

Geoffrey Bullough, (ed.), *Narrative and Dramatic Sources of Shakespeare*, vol. 5, 'The Roman Plays' (Macmillan, 1964)

> This is the standard work, containing the main sources, chiefly Plutarch's *Life of Antony* but also passages from other Roman lives by Plutarch, represented in North's translation of 1579.

T.B.L. Spencer, (ed.), *Shakespeare's Plutarch* (Penguin, 1964)

> This handy volume contains the relevant lives in North's Plutarch with passages from Shakespeare keyed into the text. It also has a brief glossary.

Criticism

Janet Adelman, *The Common Liar* (Yale University Press, 1973)

> A lucid account that, like that of Mason below, sees a disjunction between the action and the poetry but argues that this is deliberate and stresses the double and sometimes problematic view the play offers of its protagonists in love and politics.

John Russell Brown, *Shakespeare: Antony and Cleopatra: A Casebook* (Macmillan, 1968, revised edition, 1991)

> As well as containing a selection of earlier criticism and a number of reviews of the play in performance from 1849 to 1987, this volume contains an anthology of influential twentieth century criticism, starting with A.C. Bradley's much referred to lecture of 1909 (see Critical History).

John Drakakis, (ed.) *New Casebooks: Antony and Cleopatra: Contemporary Critical Essays* (Macmillan, 1994)

> A substantial introduction brings to bear the perspectives of recent theoretical approaches to the play. The essays and chapters referred to in Recent readings in Critical History can all be found in this volume.

Harley Granville Barker, *Prefaces to Shakespeare*, vol. 3 (Sidgewick & Jackson, London, 1930, reprinted by Batsford 1963 and 1972)

> A theatrical producer responsible for one of the first modern productions of the text as we have it, the author provides a defence of the play's structure as something that can work well on stage.

G. Wilson Knight, *The Imperial Theme* (Oxford University Press, London, 1931, revised edition Methuen, 1954)

> Analyses the themes and poetic structure, and presents a very positive view of the transcendent power of the love affair in the play.

H.A. Mason, *Shakespeare's Tragedies of Love* (Chatto and Windus, 1970)

> Two substantial chapters, one of which has the title 'Telling versus Shewing', take a sceptical view of the dramatic effectiveness of the poetry and argues that the play is not taken to a fully tragic conclusion.

Brian Vickers (ed.), *William Shakespeare: The Critical Heritage*, 6 vols. (Routledge, 1974)

> This is the fullest compilation of Shakespeare criticism arranged chronologically from the seventeenth century through to the nineteenth. The judgements of earlier writers (for example, those of Johnson, Coleridge and Hazlitt mentioned in Critical History) can be found here. Through use of the indices readers can construct their own account of the evolving critical response to the play. It includes notices of early performances.

100BC

100BC Caius Julius Caesar is born

75BC

75BC Pirates capture Caesar on his way to Rhodes. After paying the ransom, he hunts the kidnappers down and has them crucified

60BC

60BC The First Triumvirate (an unconstitutional arrangement) is secretly formed to rule the Roman Empire. Caesar joins forces with Crassus, a wealthy banker, and Gnaeus Pompeius (Pompey), a skillful general

59BC

59BC Caesar is elected consul. This furthers his political ambitions and gives him protection from various criminal charges

58-51BC

58-51BC Gaul is subjugated by Caesar in a campaign that borders on genocide. When Caesar arrives 3 million people live in Gaul. Within six years a million are dead and a further million enslaved. In 55 and 54BC he invades Britain

53BC

53BC Crassus, now governor of Syria, is captured by the Parthians, who kill him by pouring molten gold into his mouth

52BC

52BC Pompey is elected 'Consul without colleagues'. The Senate demands that Caesar disbands his armies

49-46BC

49-46BC Caesar crosses the river Rubicon and invades Italy. Three years of civil war ensue

48BC

48BC After losing the battle of Pharsalus Pompey flees to Egypt where he is murdered. Caesar becomes Cleopatra's lover

46BC

46BC Victory at Thapsus leaves Caesar undisputed dictator of Rome

44BC

44BC Caesar is murdered in an ostensibly Republican conspiracy headed by Brutus and Cassius. Mark Antony turns public opinion against the conspirators who are forced to flee Rome. Octavius Caesar, Julius Caesar's 19 year old adopted son, is denied his inheritance by Antony. While Antony is away fighting Brutus, Octavius Caesar becomes consul. He defeats Antony, but then makes a truce

43BC

43BC Caesar and Antony form the Second Triumvirate with Lepidus

42BC

42BC Antony defeats Cassius and then Brutus at Philippi

40BC

40BC The triumvirs divide the Mediterranean up between them. Antony gets the East (where he forms a liaison with Cleopatra), Octavius the West and Lepidus Africa

36BC

36BC Antony directs disastrous expeditions against the Parthians

32-30BC

32-30BC The Ptolemaic War. A clever propagandist, Octavius Caesar turns popular opinion against Antony and his Egyptian paramour, and defeats Antony at the battle of Actium in 31BC

30BC

30BC Alexandria falls to the Romans and Egypt becomes a Roman province

27BC

27BC Octavius Caesar becomes Emperor Augustus. His shrewd reforms lead to 250 years of stability in the Roman Empire

World events

1517 Egypt falls to the Ottoman Turks

1543 Copernicus challenges accepted views on astronomy (formulated in Ptolemaic Egypt) and is banned by the Catholic Church

1558 The French capture Calais, ending 210 years of English possession

1565 Sir John Hawkins brings tobacco to England

1576 First theatre in England opens at Shoreditch

1581 Conversion to Roman Catholicism is deemed treason in England

1582 Plague breaks out in London

1583 Newfoundland is claimed for Elizabeth I by Gilbert

1588 Spanish Armada defeated

1593-1606 Ottoman expansion into Europe halted by prolonged war with Austria

1595-1603 Tyrone's rebellion in Ireland

Shakespeare's life

1557 John Shakespeare marries Mary Arden

1564 William Shakespeare is born

1582 Shakespeare marries Anne Hathaway

1583 A daughter, Susanna, is born

1585 The twins, Hamnet and Judith, are born

late **1580s** - early **1590s** Shakespeare probably writes *Henry VI*, parts 1, 2 & 3 and *Richard III*

1592 Shakespeare acting in London

1592-4 He writes *The Comedy of Errors*

1594 Shakespeare writes exclusively for the Lord Chamberlain's Men

1595 *Two Gentlemen of Verona*, *The Taming of the Shrew* and *Love's Labours Lost* are thought to have been completed by this time. He writes *Romeo and Juliet*

Other literary works

1516 Thomas More, *Utopia*

1532 Machiavelli, *The Prince* (published posthumously)

1578 Robert Garnier, *Marc Antoine* (in French)

1579 North translates Plutarch's, *Lives of the Noble Grecians and Romans*

1590 Christopher Marlowe, *Dido, Queen of Carthage*

1592 Garnier's *Marc Antoine* translated into English

1594 Samuel Daniel, *The Tragedie of Cleopatra*

World events   Shakespeare's life   Other literary works

1596-8 *Henry IV*, parts 1 & 2 written

1596 Francis Drake
perishes on an expedition
to the West Indies

1598 First mention
of the game of cricket

1598-9 Globe Theatre built at Southwark

1599 *Henry V* completed

1600 *A Midsummer Night's Dream, Much
Ado about Nothing* and *The Merchant of
Venice* printed. *Twelfth Night* and *Julius
Caesar* probably written

1600-1 *Hamlet* written

1602 *Troilus and Cressida* probably written

1603 His company becomes the King's
Men, patronised by James I, the new king

1603 Elizabeth I dies

1604 *Othello*
performed

1604 James I, *A Counterblast to Tobacco*

1605 First version
of *King Lear*

1605 Cervantes, *Don Quixote*

1605 Discovery of
Guy Fawkes' plot to
destroy Parliament

1606 Shakespeare
writes *Macbeth*

1606 Ben Johnson, *Volpone*

1606-7 *Antony and Cleopatra*
probably written

1607 English Parliament rejects union
between England and Scotland

1608 The King's Men acquire Blackfriar's
Theatre for winter performances

1609 Tea is introduced into Europe
by the Dutch

1610 Use of the fork
for eating spreads from
Italy to England

1610 *Coriolanus* written

1611 Shakespeare retires to his house
in Stratford

1612 Last burning of heretics in England

1612 John Webster, *The White Devil*

1613 Globe Theatre burns down

1616 Shakespeare dies

1620 The Mayflower takes the Pilgrim
Fathers to Massachusetts

1677 John Dryden, *All for Love or the World
Well Lost*

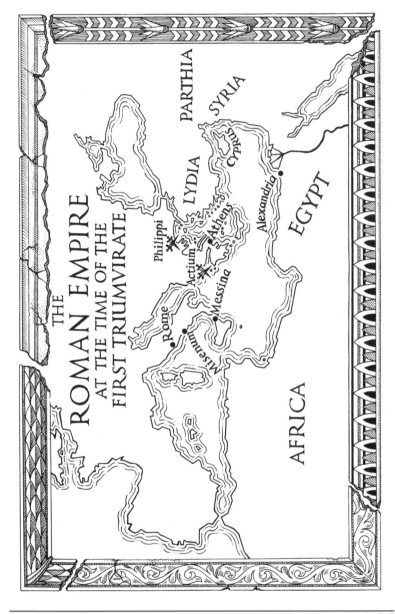

THE
ROMAN EMPIRE
AT THE TIME OF THE
FIRST TRIUMVIRATE

PARTHIA

SYRIA

LYDIA

Cyprus

Alexandria

EGYPT

Philippi

Athens

Actium

Messina

Misenum

Rome

AFRICA

anachronism from the Greek meaning refering to the wrong time, as when Cleopatra proposes playing billiards (II.5.3), a game of Shakespeare's time that had not been invented in the period in which the play is set

antithesis from the Greek meaning opposite placing. A rhetorical term describing the opposition of contrasting ideas in neighbouring sentences or clauses, using opposite or contrasting forms of words: 'In me 'tis villainy; In thee't had been good service' (II.7.74–5). The word can be used more loosely to describe a structural or thematic contrast, as when the world of Rome is deliberately contrasted with the world of Egypt in the play

conceit from the Latin meaning thought, an image that appeals to the intellect. A witty, ingenious and far fetched comparison, often extended in its application: 'Why, sir, give the gods a thankful sacrifice. When it pleaseth their deities to take the wife of a man from him, it shows to man the tailors of the earth; comforting therein, that when old robes are worn out, there are members to make new. If there were no more women but Fulvia, then had you indeed a cut, and the case to be lamented. This grief is crowned with consolation: your old smock brings forth a new petticoat; and indeed the tears live in an onion that should water this sorrow' (I.2.162–71)

figure of speech from the Latin meaning to shape, form or conceive. Any form of expression or grammar which deviates from the plainest expression of meaning; such figures may be metaphor, simile, antithesis, hyperbole, oxymoron, paradox and many others

hyperbole from the Greek, meaning excess, exaggeration. Exaggerated or extravagant language used for emphasis and not intended to be understood literally; self-conscious exaggeration: 'His legs bestrid the ocean' (V.2.82)

neoclassical from the Greek word for new and the Latin word classic; an adjective used to denote in the Renaissance, seventeenth or eighteenth centuries any literature and art that sought to conform to the rules or models of Greek or Latin antiquity. The literature of the period from 1660 to 1750 is particularly marked by this tendency. Dryden's *All for Love* (1677) is constructed on neoclassical principles, that is, it obeys the rules supposedly derived from and embodied in the masterpieces of ancient tragedy; it maintains the unities and it does not mix the genres of comedy and tragedy. Judged by neoclassical standards, *Antony and Cleopatra* is an irregular play

oxymoron from the Greek, meaning pointedly foolish. A witty paradoxical expression often containing a conjunction of opposites, like 'bitter sweet': 'Royal wench!' (II.2.231)

paradox from the Greek, meaning contrary to opinion or expectation. A seemingly self-contradictory statement, which yet is shown to be (sometimes in a surprising way) true: 'for with a wound I must be cured' (IV.14.78)

simile from the Latin meaning like. An explicit comparison, for instance: 'Those his goody eyes, / that o'er the files and musters of the the war / Have glowed like plated Mars' (I.1.2–4)

tragedy from the Greek, meaning goatsong (an unhelpful derivation). The traditional account in Aristotle's *Poetics*, written about 340BC and rediscovered in the Renaissance, stressed that it featured persons of high status undergoing a change of fortune; in the best sort of tragedy the protagonist, a person neither wholly good nor wholly bad but of moderate character like Oedipus in Sophocles's *King Oedipus* (431BC), falls from greatness through some error. Aristotle's word for error, *hamartia*, is sometimes translated as tragic flaw, but it may not be a moral flaw, simply a mistake. This error leads to catastrophe and ultimately to a recognition or self discovery and the suffering involved causes the spectators to experience pity and fear from their involvement with the tragic character resulting in a catharsis, a purgation or purification of the emotions. Many traditional discussions of the play tacitly assume such a notion of the tragic experience and effect in their account

tragicomedy a play, like *Antony and Cleopatra* that mingles elements of both tragedy and comedy (for instance, characters of high and low status) which were always kept distinct in antiquity

unities in his account of Greek tragedy in the *Poetics*, Aristotle observes that plays concentrate upon one complete action and that the plots representing this single action are bound together by a chain of cause and effect in a probable or necessary sequence, that they take place in one setting and that they tend to cover a time period of little more than one revolution of the sun. From these observations are derived the dramatic unities of action, time and place. Under classical influence they acquired a special authority in the Renaissance. The only play of Shakespeare that obeys the unities is his last play *The Tempest*

Robin Sowerby studied Classics and English at Cambridge. He now lectures in the Department of English Studies at Stirling University. He has written York Notes on Homer's *Iliad* and *Odyssey*, Virgil's *Aeneid* and Plato's *Republic*. He has edited selections from Dryden and Pope and is the author of *The Classical Legacy in Renaissance Poetry*, Longman 1994.

NOTES

York Notes Advanced (£3.99 each)

Margaret Atwood
The Handmaid's Tale

Jane Austen
Mansfield Park

Jane Austen
Persuasion

Jane Austen
Pride and Prejudice

Alan Bennett
Talking Heads

William Blake
Songs of Innocence and of Experience

Charlotte Brontë
Jane Eyre

Emily Brontë
Wuthering Heights

Geoffrey Chaucer
The Franklin's Tale

Geoffrey Chaucer
General Prologue to the Canterbury Tales

Geoffrey Chaucer
The Wife of Bath's Prologue and Tale

Joseph Conrad
Heart of Darkness

Charles Dickens
Great Expectations

John Donne
Selected Poems

George Eliot
The Mill on the Floss

F. Scott Fitzgerald
The Great Gatsby

E.M. Forster
A Passage to India

Brian Friel
Translations

Thomas Hardy
The Mayor of Casterbridge

Thomas Hardy
Tess of the d'Urbervilles

Seamus Heaney
Selected Poems from Opened Ground

Nathaniel Hawthorne
The Scarlet Letter

James Joyce
Dubliners

John Keats
Selected Poems

Christopher Marlowe
Doctor Faustus

Arthur Miller
Death of a Salesman

Toni Morrison
Beloved

William Shakespeare
Antony and Cleopatra

William Shakespeare
As You Like It

William Shakespeare
Hamlet

William Shakespeare
King Lear

William Shakespeare
Measure for Measure

William Shakespeare
The Merchant of Venice

William Shakespeare
Much Ado About Nothing

William Shakespeare
Othello

William Shakespeare
Romeo and Juliet

William Shakespeare
The Tempest

William Shakespeare
The Winter's Tale

Mary Shelley
Frankenstein

Alice Walker
The Color Purple

Oscar Wilde
The Importance of Being Earnest

Tennessee Williams
A Streetcar Named Desire

John Webster
The Duchess of Malfi

W.B. Yeats
Selected Poems

GCSE and equivalent levels (£3.50 each)

Maya Angelou
I Know Why the Caged Bird Sings

Jane Austen
Pride and Prejudice

Alan Ayckbourn
Absent Friends

Elizabeth Barrett Browning
Selected Poems

Robert Bolt
A Man for All Seasons

Harold Brighouse
Hobson's Choice

Charlotte Brontë
Jane Eyre

Emily Brontë
Wuthering Heights

Shelagh Delaney
A Taste of Honey

Charles Dickens
David Copperfield

Charles Dickens
Great Expectations

Charles Dickens
Hard Times

Charles Dickens
Oliver Twist

Roddy Doyle
Paddy Clarke Ha Ha Ha

George Eliot
Silas Marner

George Eliot
The Mill on the Floss

William Golding
Lord of the Flies

Oliver Goldsmith
She Stoops To Conquer

Willis Hall
The Long and the Short and the Tall

Thomas Hardy
Far from the Madding Crowd

Thomas Hardy
The Mayor of Casterbridge

Thomas Hardy
Tess of the d'Urbervilles

Thomas Hardy
The Withered Arm and other Wessex Tales

L.P. Hartley
The Go-Between

Seamus Heaney
Selected Poems

Susan Hill
I'm the King of the Castle

Barry Hines
A Kestrel for a Knave

Louise Lawrence
Children of the Dust

Harper Lee
To Kill a Mockingbird

Laurie Lee
Cider with Rosie

Arthur Miller
The Crucible

Arthur Miller
A View from the Bridge

Robert O'Brien
Z for Zachariah

Frank O'Connor
My Oedipus Complex and other stories

George Orwell
Animal Farm

J.B. Priestley
An Inspector Calls

Willy Russell
Educating Rita

Willy Russell
Our Day Out

J.D. Salinger
The Catcher in the Rye

William Shakespeare
Henry IV Part 1

William Shakespeare
Henry V

William Shakespeare
Julius Caesar

William Shakespeare
Macbeth

William Shakespeare
The Merchant of Venice

William Shakespeare
A Midsummer Night's Dream

William Shakespeare
Much Ado About Nothing

William Shakespeare
Romeo and Juliet

William Shakespeare
The Tempest

William Shakespeare
Twelfth Night

George Bernard Shaw
Pygmalion

Mary Shelley
Frankenstein

R.C. Sherriff
Journey's End

Rukshana Smith
Salt on the snow

John Steinbeck
Of Mice and Men

Robert Louis Stevenson
Dr Jekyll and Mr Hyde

Jonathan Swift
Gulliver's Travels

Robert Swindells
Daz 4 Zoe

Mildred D. Taylor
Roll of Thunder, Hear My Cry

Mark Twain
Huckleberry Finn

James Watson
Talking in Whispers

William Wordsworth
Selected Poems

A Choice of Poets

Mystery Stories of the Nineteenth Century including The Signalman

Nineteenth Century Short Stories

Poetry of the First World War

Six Women Poets

Chinua Achebe
Things Fall Apart

Edward Albee
Who's Afraid of Virginia Woolf?

Margaret Atwood
Cat's Eye

Jane Austen
Emma

Jane Austen
Northanger Abbey

Jane Austen
Sense and Sensibility

Samuel Beckett
Waiting for Godot

Robert Browning
Selected Poems

Robert Burns
Selected Poems

Angela Carter
Nights at the Circus

Geoffrey Chaucer
The Merchant's Tale

Geoffrey Chaucer
The Miller's Tale

Geoffrey Chaucer
The Nun's Priest's Tale

Samuel Taylor Coleridge
Selected Poems

Daniel Defoe
Moll Flanders

Daniel Defoe
Robinson Crusoe

Charles Dickens
Bleak House

Charles Dickens
Hard Times

Emily Dickinson
Selected Poems

Carol Ann Duffy
Selected Poems

George Eliot
Middlemarch

T.S. Eliot
The Waste Land

T.S. Eliot
Selected Poems

Henry Fielding
Joseph Andrews

E.M. Forster
Howards End

John Fowles
The French Lieutenant's Woman

Robert Frost
Selected Poems

Elizabeth Gaskell
North and South

Stella Gibbons
Cold Comfort Farm

Graham Greene
Brighton Rock

Thomas Hardy
Jude the Obscure

Thomas Hardy
Selected Poems

Joseph Heller
Catch-22

Homer
The Iliad

Homer
The Odyssey

Gerard Manley Hopkins
Selected Poems

Aldous Huxley
Brave New World

Kazuo Ishiguro
The Remains of the Day

Ben Jonson
The Alchemist

Ben Jonson
Volpone

James Joyce
A Portrait of the Artist as a Young Man

Philip Larkin
Selected Poems

D.H. Lawrence
The Rainbow

D.H. Lawrence
Selected Stories

D.H. Lawrence
Sons and Lovers

D.H. Lawrence
Women in Love

John Milton
Paradise Lost Bks I & II

John Milton
Paradise Lost Bks IV & IX

Thomas More
Utopia

Sean O'Casey
Juno and the Paycock

George Orwell
Nineteen Eighty-four

John Osborne
Look Back in Anger

Wilfred Owen
Selected Poems

Sylvia Plath
Selected Poems

Alexander Pope
Rape of the Lock and other poems

Ruth Prawer Jhabvala
Heat and Dust

Jean Rhys
Wide Sargasso Sea

William Shakespeare
As You Like It

William Shakespeare
Coriolanus

William Shakespeare
Henry IV Pt 1

William Shakespeare
Henry V

William Shakespeare
Julius Caesar

William Shakespeare
Macbeth

William Shakespeare
Measure for Measure

William Shakespeare
A Midsummer Night's Dream

William Shakespeare
Richard II

William Shakespeare
Richard III

William Shakespeare
Sonnets

William Shakespeare
The Taming of the Shrew

William Shakespeare
Twelfth Night

William Shakespeare
The Winter's Tale

George Bernard Shaw
Arms and the Man

George Bernard Shaw
Saint Joan

Muriel Spark
The Prime of Miss Jean Brodie

John Steinbeck
The Grapes of Wrath

John Steinbeck
The Pearl

Tom Stoppard
Arcadia

Tom Stoppard
*Rosencrantz and Guildenstern
are Dead*

Jonathan Swift
*Gulliver's Travels and The
Modest Proposal*

Alfred, Lord Tennyson
Selected Poems

W.M. Thackeray
Vanity Fair

Virgil
The Aeneid

Edith Wharton
The Age of Innocence

Tennessee Williams
Cat on a Hot Tin Roof

Tennessee Williams
The Glass Menagerie

Virginia Woolf
Mrs Dalloway

Virginia Woolf
To the Lighthouse

William Wordsworth
Selected Poems

Metaphysical Poets

York Notes – the Ultimate Literature Guides

York Notes are recognised as the best literature study guides.
If you have enjoyed using this book and have found it useful, you
can now order others directly from us – simply follow the ordering
instructions below.

HOW TO ORDER

Decide which title(s) you require and then order in one of the following
ways:

Booksellers
All titles available from good bookstores.

By post
List the title(s) you require in the space provided overleaf,
select your method of payment, complete your name and
address details and return your completed order form and
payment to:

> *Addison Wesley Longman Ltd*
> *PO BOX 88*
> *Harlow*
> *Essex CM19 5SR*

By phone
Call our Customer Information Centre on 01279 623923 to
place your order, quoting mail number: HEYN1.

By fax
Complete the order form overleaf, ensuring you fill in your
name and address details and method of payment, and fax it
to us on 01279 414130.

By e-mail
E-mail your order to us on awlhe.orders@awl.co.uk listing
title(s) and quantity required and providing full name and
address details as requested overleaf. Please quote mail
number: HEYN1. Please do not send credit card details by
e-mail.

York Notes Order Form

Titles required:

Quantity	Title/ISBN	Price

Sub total _____

Please add £2.50 postage & packing _____

(*P & P is free for orders over £50*) _____

Total _____

Mail no: HEYN1

Your Name _____

Your Address _____

_____

Postcode _____ Telephone _____

Method of payment

☐ I enclose a cheque or a P/O for £_____ made payable to Addison Wesley Longman Ltd

☐ Please charge my Visa/Access/AMEX/Diners Club card

Number _____ Expiry Date _____

Signature _____ Date _____

(please ensure that the address given above is the same as for your credit card)

Prices and other details are correct at time of going to press but may change without notice. All orders are subject to status.

☐ *Please tick this box if you would like a complete listing of Longman Study Guides (suitable for GCSE and A-level students)*

York Press

Longman

Addison
Wesley
Longman